F

INDUSTRIAL VALLEY

Jack Gieck

EARLY AKRON'S

INDUSTRIAL

VALLEY

A History of the Cascade Locks

Jack Gieck

KENT STATE UNIVERSITY PRESS

Kent, Ohio

© 2008 by The Kent State University Press, Kent, Ohio 44242

All rights reserved

Library of Congress Catalog Card Number 2007038504

ISBN 978-0-87338-928-0

Manufactured in the United States of America

12 11 10 09 08   5 4 3 2 1

Library of Congress Cataloging-in-Publication Data

Gieck, Jack.

Early Akron's industrial valley : a history of the Cascade Locks / Jack Gieck.

p.   cm.

Includes bibliographical references.

ISBN 978-0-87338-928-0 (pbk. : alk. paper) ∞

1. Canals—Ohio—History.   2. Industries—Ohio—Akron—History.

3. Entrepreneurs—Ohio—Akron—History.   I. Title.

HE395.O34G537 2008

386'.480977136—dc22   2007038504

British Library Cataloging-in-Publication data are available.

Contents

MAPS

PREFACE

More than a year ago I started working on a brochure that would be a brief history of Akron's Cascade Locks—the staircase of sixteen locks that was the last and steepest mile of these primitive hydraulic elevators that lifted Ohio & Erie Canal boats from the level of Lake Erie in Cleveland to the Akron summit 38 miles to the south. But when I began researching the subject, I realized that the parallel Cascade Race, rushing down this same precipitous slope and spawning a string of industries between the two waterways, constituted a tale that wouldn't fit into a mere brochure. As an engineer, I developed even more enthusiasm for the project after getting acquainted with the entrepreneurs whose drive and ingenuity built this thriving string of mills, as well as cupola furnaces, iron foundries, a brewery, a distillery, and other industries all operating on water power.

What follows is a story of the successes and failures of these pioneers—how their efforts contributed to intense competition between the young community of Cascade and the well-established Akron, and how this rivalry was put to rest with the arrival of a second canal, the Pennsylvania & Ohio, through downtown Akron, paving the way for the city's future position as the Rubber Capital of the World.

With sincere thanks to Bridget Garvin and to Bruce Norton for their considerable contributions, as well as those of artist-historian Chuck Ayers, who made new maps. Thanks to Steve Griebling for loaning Carl Griebling's mill model for use in this book. Thanks also to George Knepper, Siegfried Buehrling, Joe Jesensky, Virginia Wojno-Forney, Doug Hausknecht, Al Brion, Carl Ehmann, Charles Snyder, John Henry Vance, and other historians.

JACK GIECK

EARLY AKRON'S

INDUSTRIAL VALLEY

Akron is on the Continental Divide. Rain falling on the north side of town flows north into the St. Lawrence watershed. Rain landing in south Akron goes south into the Mississippi basin. You can actually see the water dividing and flowing both ways at the point where the Portage Lakes feeder enters the Ohio & Erie Canal across from Young's Tavern on Manchester Road in south Akron. Water flowing to the left goes north through downtown Akron and Cuyahoga Falls into the Cuyahoga River and out into Lake Erie, from which it runs northeast through Lake Ontario, up the St. Lawrence River, and out into the North Atlantic Ocean. Water going to the right flows south into the Tuscarawas River and from there finds its way down to the Ohio River, a tributary of the Mississippi, which then carries it another 600 miles south and out into the Gulf of Mexico. Akron sits at the top of the ridge dividing the two continental watersheds—at the summit.

The barrier was well known to Native Americans long before Europeans arrived in North America. For hundreds of years Woodland Indians traveling south on the Cuyahoga River from Lake Erie lifted their canoes out of the water at Old Portage, carrying them up over the summit (from which Summit County takes its name) along 9 miles of the Portage Path before descending to the Tuscarawas River to continue their journey.

The north side of the Akron summit is much steeper than the south side. It is so steep, in fact, that when Ohio's landmark Canal Act was passed in February 1825, canal engineers discovered that they would have to build sixteen locks to raise canal boats 149 feet in this last mile of the 38-mile trip from Cleveland, creating a staircase of locks. (This is why canal boats from the north often spent the night in the basin below Lock 15 before beginning the tortuous ascent, loading up on food and supplies in the morning after the Mustill Store opened.)

But what engineers viewed as an obstacle, Dr. Eliakim Crosby of Middlebury seized on as an entrepreneurial opportunity. He recognized that terrain this steep could be used to generate massive amounts of waterpower if an ample supply of water could be found. (Canal water couldn't be used since it was needed to operate the cascade of locks.) But Crosby conceived a bold plan that would ultimately transform the site below Lock 5 into a dynamic industrial valley rivaling sites in England created by the Industrial Revolution.

Within a decade after Crosby implemented his plan, the valley came alive with several flour mills, a woolen mill, a furniture factory, five iron furnaces, and a distillery. The same water flowed out of one factory and into the next one, and all of them were powered by gravity. The site is preserved today from Lock 10 through Lock 16 as Akron's Cascade Locks Park, developed by the Cascade Locks Park Association and operated by Metro Parks, Serving Summit County in cooperation with the City of Akron.

. . .

Eliakim Crosby arrived in Middlebury about 1820. Born in Litchfield, Connecticut, in 1779, he was well educated and taught school until he was twenty-seven years old, when, in 1806, he moved to Buffalo and studied medicine. After completing his internship, he settled in Simco, Ontario, where he opened a medical practice and married Marcia Beemer in 1810. But when the British invaded the United States during the War of 1812 and Crosby entered the U.S. Army as a surgeon, the British confiscated his Canadian property, which forced him to return to the United States.

Dr. Crosby continued to practice medicine after arriving in Middlebury, a village bordering the Little Cuyahoga River along today's Case Avenue north of East Market. The ambitious doctor built a small iron furnace on the river in Middlebury. Since his medical practice was limited to a handful of families, he was exploring other sources of income. Running a major canal through his hometown, where he already had a business, would invite prosperity. Because Middlebury was on one of several possible canal routes over the Continental Divide, Crosby and other community activists lobbied for the canal.

But General Simon Perkins of Warren, a surveyor and an agent for the Connecticut Land Company, had other ideas. In addition to representing the land company, Perkins was privately speculating in land. Using state records, he acquired a substantial amount of property simply by paying modest amounts of past-due taxes on the land. He had, in fact, by 1825, amassed 1,003 acres at a total cost of $4.07. Perkins's properties were located 2 miles west of Middlebury, adjacent to property owned by settler Paul Williams, in an area that would become downtown Akron.

Akron did not exist when the Canal Act was passed in 1825. Northeast Ohio was still a wilderness. In all of Ohio there were fewer than 300,000 people, about the population of greater Akron today. In what is now the Akron area there were only three settlers. As Henry Howe explains in his *Historical Collections of Ohio,* "In 1811, Paul Williams, Amos and Miner Spicer came from New London, Connecticut, and settled in the vicinity of Akron, at which time there was no other white settlement between here and Sandusky." In fact, one of the objectives of Ohio's Canal Act was to encourage the settlement of the northeastern part of the state.

Perkins persuaded Williams to combine their properties and lay out a town, one comprised of 172 acres, the majority owned by Perkins. When they registered it in the county seat of Ravenna, they called their town Akron, derived from a Greek word meaning "high." In a skillful political move, Perkins had the town plat drawn with a canal running through the center of the village. And to clinch the deal, he deeded a third of the town lots to the state. This, together with Perkins's vigorous lobbying in Columbus, was irresistible to the canal commissioners, who adopted the route through Akron.

Undaunted, Crosby, a clever politician as well as innovator, went to see Perkins, asking the general to partner with him on what Perkins first thought was a wildly ambitious scheme. Crosby proposed that they purchase water rights to the Little Cuyahoga River in Middlebury and build a diversion dam at the foot of Bank Street. From this dam they would "build a river," a 2-mile-long millrace that would run west along the rim of the Little Cuyahoga Valley, turn south down what would later become Akron's Main Street, and then go west down what would be called Mill Street, pouring its contents into the hydraulics of a gristmill that Crosby would build on the edge of the canal at Lock 5 (on the present site of the Radisson Hotel). After turning the machinery in Crosby's mill, the effluent water (the tail race gushing from the mammoth mill) would flow down the precipitous slope becoming a new millrace running parallel to the canal (and through property that Perkins already owned). Crosby contended that this would attract other industries into the valley. But Perkins remained unconvinced, and it would take years for him to change his mind.

Meanwhile, work on the canal got under way. The Ohio & Erie Canal between Akron and Cleveland was dug by workers who had learned their trade building New York's 174-mile Erie Canal. Running from Buffalo on Lake Erie to Albany on the Hudson River, the canal had opened in 1825 and was a resounding success. Having completed that waterway, which connected ports on Lake Erie with New York City and East Coast markets, these experienced workers migrated westward to build the Ohio & Erie Canal.

Working from dawn to dusk, thousands of men lining the Cuyahoga River Valley dug this first 38 miles of canal from Akron to Cleveland in less than two years. As described by historian George Knepper,

> Some were local farmers who did the work in the off-season, but the majority were immigrant Irish and German workers. . . . Poor, uneducated, and passionate, the Irish were often social outcasts ridiculed by "people of quality." Yet it was their labor, often twelve hours a day in stinking ooze up to the waist, that built the canals. Thirty cents a day and a gill of whiskey was their usual wage until competition for their labor pushed wages up in the 1830s. Working conditions left them vulnerable to malaria, typhoid, and other scourges. Undernourished and overtired, living in squalor, they were an easy prey for

epidemics such as a cholera epidemic of 1832 that killed hundreds. Alcohol, accidents, and murderous fights took many lives, and many a worker was placed in an unmarked grave along the ditch. Occasionally a worker, killed in mysterious circumstances, was buried in the canal bed. (*Ohio and Its People,* 154)

The "Ohio Canal," as it was called, would be 309 miles long, running from Cleveland to Portsmouth, from Lake Erie to the Ohio River. Not a shortcut, it was to be an inland transportation system that would permit farmers (and, later, manufacturers) to ship their products to waiting markets on the East Coast by way of Lake Erie and the Erie Canal, or to settlements along the Ohio and Mississippi Rivers from Cincinnati to St. Louis to the Port of New Orleans.

The canal was not merely a ditch. As specified by the canal engineers, the canal's profile was to be a "prism" not less than 26 feet wide at the bottom, with sloping sides, to provide 40 feet of width at the water level, which was to be no less than 4 feet in depth. In practice, the canal was dug five to 12 feet deep, having a width that varied from 50 to 150 feet. To make them as waterproof as possible, the banks and bottom were lined with clay after grubbing and clearing the banks of any porous stone or vegetation that might contribute to leakage, which would lower the canal's water level and cause boats to run aground.

Between Akron and Cleveland the canal mostly paralleled the Cuyahoga River, with a 10-foot towpath running between the two

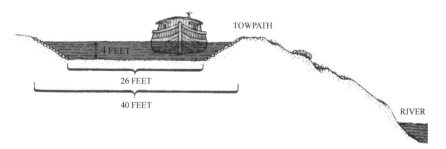

The canal prism, or cross-section of the canal, as specified by canal engineers. (Drawn by the author and based on an illustration by Carl Sachs)

waterways. Together with stone masons and other artisans, the workers also built a total of forty-four locks to raise the boats 395 feet from the level of Lake Erie to the Akron Summit at Lock 1. Almost 40 percent of that rise would occur in the last mile, from Lock 16 to Lock 1.

Launching such a mammoth project was a major happening, and the locals basked in the attention they received. People from as far as Columbus came to participate in the festivities. The *Ravenna Western Courier and Western Public Advertiser* sent a reporter to Akron's Lock 3 on September 10, 1825, to cover the laying of the first lock stone on the Ohio & Erie Canal. He described the protracted ceremonies a week later under the headline, "Ohio Canal Celebration":

> The Ceremonies of laying the First Lock Stone of the Ohio Canal were more attractive and imposing than was generally anticipated— that so short a notice could have attracted such a concourse. . . . People from different and distant parts continued to assemble until 11 or 12 o'clock when the Middlebury Lodge, in connection with several visiting lodges, and many visiting brethren, together with a great number of Ladies, and a numerous collection of private citizens, were formed into a procession, and under the appointed Marshals, marched to the line of the Canal.
>
> Mr. E. Torry, the Grand Marshal, ascended the Stone and delivered a short but emphatic address; an Ode was sung by a choir consisting of twenty-seven females and about an equal number of males, accompanied by instruments led by Adaph Whittlesey. The Rev. E. Williams then made an appropriate and impressive prayer; invoking the blessings of Heaven on the work and on all present— and imploring its prospering favors on the State and its great undertaking. . . .

The stonemasons who built the Cascade Locks were commonly members of the Fraternal Order of Freemasonry, hence the formal Masonic ceremonies.

> The Stone was then raised, and all who felt so disposed, deposited mementos underneath. During this part of the ceremony, the

singers were performing an Ode . . . which had the most solemn and grand effect. . . . After the usual ceremony of the *Cora, Wine & Oil* and a benediction by the Grand Master, Dr. E. Crosby stepped upon the Stone and delivered an address which had been prepared for the occasion.

We were at too great a distance from the orator to hear distinctly . . . but we have been informed by those who did hear (and those in whose taste and judgment we have confidence) that its style was neat, and that its incidents were well selected.

The content of entrepreneur, politician, and salesman Dr. Eliakim Crosby's speech was probably less important than Crosby making his presence known. After all, he had his eye on the future.

. . .

The dimensions of Lock 3 were the same as all of the others yet to be built. Designed to pass canal boats that were usually 70 to 80 feet long and 14 feet wide, locks were 90 feet long and 15 feet wide. The walls were built with huge rectangular blocks of cut sandstone, some weighing hundreds of pounds, and each was sawed by hand at one of several local stone quarries. It was a tight fit for some boats whose wooden fenders on the sides of the hull exceeded the 14-foot width specification. To protect the keel of the boats, the floor of each lock was lined with heavy wooden timbers. These can still be seen today on the bottom of some of the Cascade Locks. They remain well preserved underwater after nearly two centuries.

Locks were closed at each end by heavy wooden "whaler gates" (so called because they resembled the doors on whaling ships that were opened to drag whale carcasses aboard). Made of two plies of wood planks running at right angles to each other, these gates hung on wrought-iron hinges and closed in a V pointing upstream so that the "head" of water pressure against them could not push them open. Boatmen opened and closed them using heavy wooden handles called "balance beams," or "sweeps," that were eight to 9 feet long.

In raising (or lowering) a boat from one level to another, the locks operated like hydraulic elevators, but they worked entirely by gravity.

A typical canal lock with sandstone walls and leaking wooden gates. This one, at Peninsula, has an aqueduct behind it. (Canal Society of Ohio)

Near the bottom of each gate was a wicket (also called a butterfly valve or paddle), which was opened and closed by means of an iron control lever that stuck up above the top of the gate. To lift a boat from one level to another, a boatman (or a lockmaster, though rarely in this part of Ohio) would first drain the lock by opening the wickets in the lower gates. When the water level in the lock had gone down far enough to match the downstream water level, the lower gates were opened and the boat was drawn inside. After the lower gates and their wickets were closed, the ones in the upper gates were opened, filling the lock to the upstream level. The upper gates were then opened and the boat continued on the canal route. Since the mules had to be unhitched while this was going on, it took about twenty minutes for a skilled crew to negotiate each lock, and longer for novices.

Since most of the Cascade Locks had a lift of 10 feet (see table on p. 10), water pouring into the lock through the butterfly valves in the upper gate—well above the heads of any passengers or crew who happened to be on deck at the time—presented a problem. To prevent this torrent of water from drenching those on deck below, each of the Cascade Locks was constructed with an internal sluiceway. On one of the lock walls just above the upper gate and below the waterline was a 2-foot-square opening covered by a sliding wooden trapdoor. When this hatch was opened, upstream water would go around the gate, flowing through a channel between the lock stones and coming out beside the boat below the waterline. This engineering "trick" made for dryer and

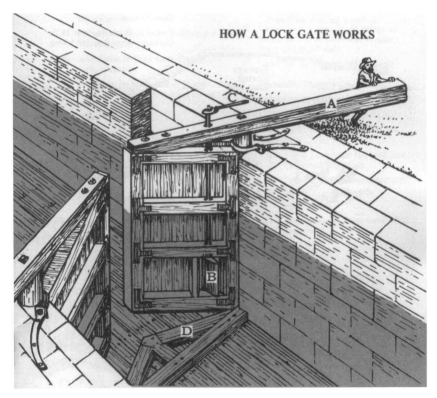

A lock tender opens a gate by pushing against the sweep, or lock handle (A). He has drained the lock by opening the butterfly valve, or paddle (B), by means of an iron handle (C), at the top of the gate, which closes against the lock sill (D). (James and Margot Jackson, *The Colorful Era of the Ohio Canal*)

Lifts of the Cascade Locks

Lock 1	10'	Lock 5	10'	Lock 9	10'	Lock 13	10'
Lock 2	10'	Lock 6	10'	Lock 10	10'	Lock 14	10'
Lock 3	8'	Lock 7	8'	Lock 11	10'	Lock 15	10'
Lock 4	12'	Lock 8	10'	Lock 12	10'	Lock 16	11'

happier passengers and crews. (The remains of these sluiceways can be seen at the south end of the lock walls in Cascade Locks Park.)

Providing sufficient water to operate the canal proved to be an ongoing problem. For a lift of 10 feet, operating a lock would release more than 13,000 cubic feet of water—about 100,000 gallons irrevocably lost downstream. To provide for a passage of 100 boats a day (generally considered the maximum a lockmaster could handle) an average flow of 1,500 cubic feet per minute from a source above the lock would have to be maintained. But, after taking into account evaporation and leakage, canal engineers figured that at least ten times this amount would be required. With a uniform flow of traffic in both directions, it would be possible to double the number of boats passing through a lock using the same volume of water; however, as the second Annual Report of the Canal Commissioners observed in 1824, "it would be extremely vexatious to compel a boat to wait until one should arrive to pass in the opposite direction."

The water for operating the locks in the Akron area came from (and still comes from) the Portage Lakes, which were dammed and enlarged for the purpose, and there may have been additional sources from springs under Summit Lake. Nevertheless, between Akron and Cleveland, three feeders from the Cuyahoga River had to be built to make up for leakage. During the years the canal was in operation, the state employed workmen who wore backpacks full of straw and who walked the towpath to plug leaks made by burrowing muskrats and groundhogs.

Finishing the canal segment from Cleveland to Akron in less than two years was a remarkable accomplishment for men whose only tools were shovels and wheelbarrows and mule-drawn carts (which hauled away the dirt and usually dumped it on the side of the canal opposite the towpath to form the "berm," the opposite wall of the

Canal builders' only tools were shovels, scoops, wheelbarrows, and mule-drawn carts. (George Eastman House, Rochester)

canal channel). In another five short years, all 309 miles of the canal from Cleveland on Lake Erie to Portsmouth on the Ohio River would be completed, including 151 lift locks and seven guard locks. For historical comparison, building the Grand Canal of China (admittedly three times as long but with no locks) took a thousand years—from the sixth century B.C. until 610 A.D.

While canal workers were digging the channel and building the locks, local entrepreneurs in Akron, Cleveland, and the village of Boston were establishing boatyards where artisans with other skills were busily constructing the first vessels to ply the new waterway. Canal boats were not barges. Barges have flat bottoms and no engines or rudders. Since canal craft had rudders and curved wooden hulls and were self-propelled, albeit by three mules in tandem (generating almost three horsepower), they qualify as boats.

. . .

On June 27, 1827, the small crowd at the Wheeler Brothers Boatyard near Akron's Exchange Street buzzed with anticipation. A cheer went up as the wooden blocks were knocked out from greased skids and

A boat in the dry dock of W. J. Payne's boatyard in Akron. The heavy wooden fenders on the sides of the boat protect the hull as it passes through locks. (Canal Visitor Center, CVNP)

the *State of Ohio* slid sideways into the canal basin above Lock 2, creating a small tidal wave that splashed up on the opposite bank. The first boat on the Ohio & Erie Canal had been launched, and to the surprise of doubters in the crowd, it floated. Just days later on July 3, Governor Allen Trimble would arrive by stagecoach from Columbus, together with the secretary of state and several canal commissioners, to witness the opening of the Akron-Cleveland section of the canal.

The assembled crowd suffered through barely audible speeches (over the noise from the bypass channel waterfall next to the lock) by each of the visiting dignitaries until Captain Henry Richards and steersman John Sterns poled the festively decorated *State of Ohio* into Akron's Lock 2, where the distinguished guests clambered aboard the vessel. Accompanied by noisy band music with a heavy percussion section, a pair of crew members, one on either side of the canal, shoved their backs against the heavy wooden sweeps to close the upper gates and then walked the length of the lock to the lower gates to turn the pair of iron control handles that opened the butterfly valves at the base of the gates. As the water drained out of the lock, gushing downstream out of the open butterfly valves, the boat descended like an elevator, dropping 10 feet to the lower water level. The crewmen then opened the lower gates.

For this signal occasion mules would not do. Instead, Job Harrington's carefully groomed black horses were hitched up, given a persuasive prod, and the first boat on the Ohio & Erie Canal headed north as the throng lining the banks drank toasts to the new era at hand. The *State of Ohio* descended another 8 feet at Lock 3, a whopping 12 feet at Lock 4, and another 10 feet at Lock 5. With each step, the crew improved its performance. By the time the boat reached Lock 9 at Market Street, only some in the crowd were still following on the towpath to watch the action; it would take hours for the boat's inaugural descent down the grand staircase of the Cascade Locks from Lock 10 to Lock 16.

By the following morning, the *State of Ohio* had reached the new boatyard at Boston, where it was joined by the *Allen Trimble,* which sported a loaded brass cannon at its bow to greet its sister ship and salute the governor for whom the flagship boat was named. Amid cheers and answering cannon volleys from the shore, Bostonians watched the procession fade out of sight to the north. Six miles south of Cleveland's flats, the pair met the *Pioneer,* and as the stately flotilla proceeded down the Cuyahoga Valley into the center of Cleveland, it was greeted by even larger rejoicing crowds well supplied with what became the twin trademarks of canal celebrations: gunpowder and alcohol.

More canal boats would be built in Akron than in any other community in Ohio's entire 813-mile canal system. Initially, the boatyards built freight boats. Riding low in the water, freight boats were capable of hauling 50 to 80 tons of cargo. These vessels had three cabins on deck with two open cargo holds in between. The rear cabin was the largest, since it housed the captain and his whole family (indeed, some canal families had as many as ten children). The forward cabin at the bow was where the rest of the crew slept, and the center cabin was the stable for the spare mule team. A full crew consisted of the captain, a steersman who handled the rudder, a bowsman who assisted the lockmaster (if there was one), and a mule driver, or "muleskinner," who was often a teenage boy.

A freight boat pulled by three mules in tandem, hitched to a single towline, is driven by a muleskinner. (Author's collection)

State boats, operated for canal maintenance, had no middle cabin since they operated only during daylight hours. On some line boats, the cargo holds between the cabins were closed in to accommodate both freight and passengers. Seventeen-year-old Cyrus Parker, a student at Dartmouth College, kept a journal during his passage on an Ohio & Erie line boat in June 1835: "The forward part of the boat is the gentlemen's cabin, about 10 by 5; then the main part of the boat for the freight, where are also stowed the midship passengers; then in the after part of the boat, the dining room, perhaps 10 feet square, with a kitchen closet adjoining. Our little cabin was fitted most ingeniously with berths for ten persons, but so contracted were the limits appropriated for each that he could only draw himself onto his shelf lengthwise and lie without stirring for fear of a fall or a broken head" (Lane, *Fifty Years*).

Passenger packets, introduced later in the century, were much sleeker in appearance and could carry fifty to seventy-five passengers (now including women). Because they rarely tied up, operating around the clock, these boats carried a larger crew. In addition to the captain and a matron for the lady passengers, packets usually had two drivers, two steersmen, and a cook. One passenger line advertised, "Cleveland to Portsmouth, 308 miles in 80 hours." Passenger fares were less than two cents a mile, half a cent of which went for tolls.

Following is a log of expenses, including meals, kept by the Reverend B. W. Chidlaw during a journey of more than a thousand miles he made from New York to Cincinnati in 1836. On that trip, which took about a month, he sailed up the Hudson River by steamboat to Albany and then boarded an Erie Canal boat across New York state to Buffalo. From there he took a lake steamer to Cleveland, where he boarded an Ohio & Erie Canal packet that took him from Cleveland to Portsmouth. He finished his journey down the Ohio River to Cincinnati on a riverboat.

Leg	Via	Cost	Miles
New York–Albany	steamboat	$2.00	100
Albany–Utica	stage/canal	1.50	110
Utica–Buffalo	canal	3.75	254
Buffalo–Cleveland	steamboat	2.50	193
Cleveland–Portsmouth	canal	4.00	309
Portsmouth–Cincinnati	steamboat	1.00	100

Passenger packets began running on the Ohio & Erie Canal within a decade after its completion. The hours spent going through the Cascade Locks in the summertime were dreary ones for some passengers. Former president John Quincy Adams wrote about his experiences on a packet in 1843:

So much humanity crowded into such a compass was a trial such as I had never before experienced, and my heart sunk within me when, squeezing into this pillory, I reflected that I am to pass three or four days in it. . . . The most uncomfortable part of our navigation is caused by the careless and unskillful steering of the boat in and through the locks, which seem to be numberless, upwards of two hundred of them on the canal. The boat scarcely escapes a heavy thump on entering every one of them. She strikes and grazes against their sides, and staggers along like a stumbling nag.

. . .

The effects of completing those first 38 miles of the canal from Akron to Cleveland were felt immediately. Until 1827, Cleveland merchants had sold about a thousand barrels of flour to merchants in New York. But in 1828, the first full year of operation of this canal segment, they sold 250,000 barrels, suddenly transforming Cleveland from a sleepy little village into a major lake port.

A number of small lock mills had already sprouted along the route. With a license from the state, millers could use the modest drop in water level at a lock (usually 6–10 feet) to generate enough water-power to turn a pair of millstones. Every lock had a bypass channel, or wasteway, that detoured excess water around the lock during periods of light traffic so the water wouldn't flow over the tops of the gates—or, worse, wash them out during a storm. The millers fed some of the water from this stream over or under a waterwheel (later through a vertical rotor) to turn its milling machinery. Barrels of flour could be loaded directly onto boats in the adjacent canal, and to facilitate loading, some mills actually straddled the canal.

It was probably facts like these that caused Simon Perkins to reconsider Eliakim Crosby's bold scheme. He was also aware that his town, Akron, wasn't growing very fast. Moreover, since he owned nearly all of the canal land from Lock 1 through Lock 17, he would profit by selling pieces of it to any new businesses that resulted from Crosby's venture. So, joined by Judge Leicester King, Perkins put $6,000 into Crosby's enterprise in 1831. Not long after, he collected $8,000 from Crosby for 300 acres of land on which the doctor intended to found his village of Cascade.

As Karl Grismer recounts in *Akron and Summit County,* "To stimulate development of the settlement, Crosby . . . donated choice lots on [what would later become] the northwest corner of Howard and Market to James Baldwin, of Amsterdam, New York, as an inducement to build a two-story hotel. It was completed in 1832, and Baldwin leased it to Willard W. Stevens, who named it the Cascade House." The doctor gave two more choice lots to Seth Iredell, who built a two-story structure in which he opened his Cascade Store late in 1832.

Crosby's 2-mile millrace was finished the same year. It was dug (actually, a portion of the waterway near Middlebury had to be blasted out

Eliakim Crosby's Stone Mill at Lock 5. (University of Akron Archives)

of bedrock) by hundreds of Irish canal workers who had returned to Akron to participate in Crosby's project after having worked their way south, building the remaining 270 miles of the canal to Portsmouth. Again, with perseverance, the Irishmen completed "Crosby's Ditch" in a single year. Stone masons who had built the Cascade Locks also returned to construct what would be known by generations of Akronites as the "Old Stone Mill," Crosby's five-story gristmill at Lock 5. It was the tallest structure in Akron.

Dr. Crosby's mill (at the foot of what would be called Mill Street) went into operation in 1832. With its four sets of imported French burrstones turned by the water flowing from the new dam on the Little Cuyahoga River, the Stone Mill had ten times the capacity of a lock mill. As Crosby had predicted, the effluent water discharged out of his mill became the Cascade Race, offering a dependable source of waterpower to potential entrepreneurs downstream. At the bottom

Overleaf: Route of Eliakim Crosby's 2-mile millrace from a dam on the Little Cuyahoga River to his Stone Mill at Lock 5 on the Ohio & Erie Canal. (Map by Chuck Ayers)

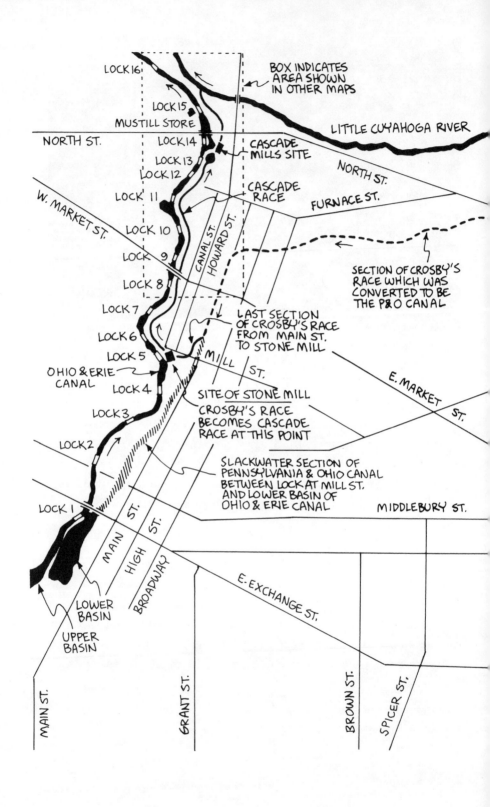

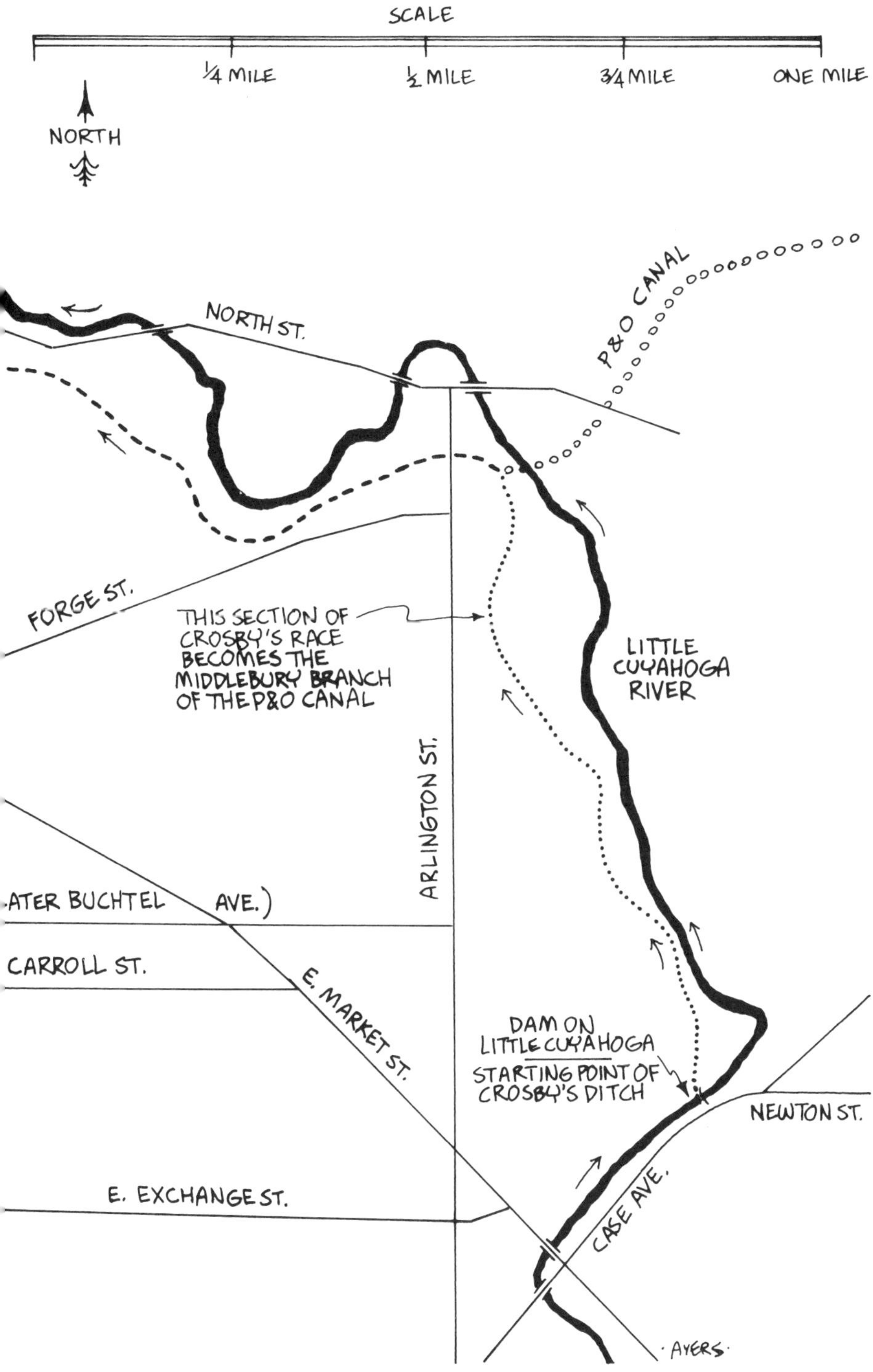

SCALE

¼ MILE   ½ MILE   ¾ MILE   ONE MILE

NORTH

P&O CANAL

NORTH ST.

FORGE ST.

THIS SECTION OF
CROSBY'S RACE
BECOMES THE
MIDDLEBURY BRANCH
OF THE P&O CANAL

LITTLE
CUYAHOGA
RIVER

ARLINGTON ST.

ATER BUCHTEL   AVE.)

CARROLL ST.

E. MARKET ST.

DAM ON
LITTLE CUYAHOGA
STARTING POINT OF
CROSBY'S DITCH

NEWTON ST.

E. EXCHANGE ST.

CASE AVE.

· AYERS ·

of the steep slope at Lock 14, the Cascade Race disappeared into an arched brick and cut-stone tunnel 558 feet long, which poured into the Little Cuyahoga River between Locks 14 and 15. The entrance to the tunnel, originally 11 feet wide by 8 feet high, can still be seen.

The race paralleled the canal on the east side, close enough that a mill or factory could be constructed to fill the space between the two waterways—using the Cascade Race on the east side of the building to turn its machinery while unloading its product directly onto canal boats on the west side. Within a year, four new enterprises bought pieces of the property that Crosby had purchased from Perkins along the Cascade Race.

A small community known as Cascade took root in the area, some of it on the west side of the canal. By July 1833 Cascade had a population of 128, including the family of Eliakim Crosby, who had moved from Middlebury into a new home overlooking the canal and his Cascade Race at the foot of Beech Street (misspelled on some maps as Beach Street) between Locks 10 and 11 in what is now Cascade Locks Park.

Soon thereafter, David and Jesse Allen of Coventry Township bought a site for $7,000 and built a wool carding and spinning mill on Cherry Street near Lock 6. The brothers were in partnership with Reuben Mc-Millan of Galway, New York. A third Allen brother, Jacob, would later open a cloth dressing mill at North Street. Akron became noted for its woolen industry. Indeed, Simon Perkins's son, Simon Jr., raised sheep on the land surrounding the famous Stone Mansion his father built for him in 1837. The younger Perkins's wool business was run for several years by famed abolitionist John Brown, who had earned a reputation as one of the best wool judges in the United States. Their partnership was known as Perkins & Brown.

While the Allens were building their woolen mill, Hiram Payne was building a distillery at Beech Street, one with a capacity of producing two barrels of whiskey a day. According to Karl Grismer, "Its construction was hailed by the community. In those days, no town was worthy of a name unless it had a plant where grain could be converted into the liquid staff of life."

To the chagrin of Middlebury residents, William J. Hart (son of the town's founder, Captain Joseph Hart) proved to be another apostate, pulling up stakes to build a small blast furnace in Cascade at the foot of what would be called Furnace Street, which ended between Locks 11 and 12. He called his enterprise The Aetna. A second iron furnace was built by Charles W. Howard and Jonathan F. Fenn. They erected their furnace at the foot of Market Street, which ended at the pair of waterways, since a Market Street bridge wouldn't be built until 1834. The enterprising pair also took over Seth Iredell's Cascade Store.

Both of the new ironworks on the Cascade Race were cupola furnaces, small blast furnaces that smelted iron from its ore—a metallurgical process that has changed very little since its invention in Egypt or Asia Minor about 4,000 years ago. The furnaces in early Akron were pyramid-shaped chimneys about three stories high and were built of firebrick. To smelt iron in them, a wood fire was built in the bottom and the raw materials—iron oxide ore, charcoal, and limestone—were dumped from a high wooden platform, or bridge, by wheelbarrow into an opening near the top. Making one ton of iron required 2.5 tons of iron ore, 180 bushels of charcoal, and 1.5 tons of limestone.

The fire in the bottom of the furnace was fanned by a blast of air to raise the temperature to nearly 3,000 degrees, causing the carbon in the charcoal to combine with the oxygen in the iron oxide ore and release raw iron. For thousands of years this air blast had been produced by blowing on the fire with leather bellows. But the furnaces in Akron's industrial valley were nineteenth-century state-of-the-art: a waterwheel worked a pair of huge reciprocating wooden cylinders that pumped a heavy, continuous blast of pressurized air into the base of the fire through a tapered blowpipe nozzle called a tuyere. Molten iron accumulated in the bottom of the furnace, which was periodically tapped; the glowing molten iron ran out in a shower of sparks, and the limestone flux, which contained impurities, floated to the top to be hauled away as slag.

The first cupola furnace in the area was built in Middlebury in 1816 by Aaron Norton and William Laird. A year later the partnership opened a foundry, an iron casting facility, at a new location known since then as Old Forge. Most of the Middlebury iron was used to make nails to build farmhouses and plows to work the land. One early plow manufacturer in Middlebury was Eliakim Crosby.

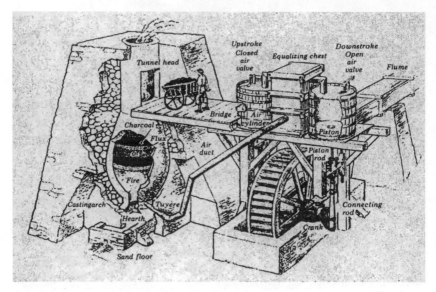

A cupola furnace was loaded by wheelbarrow with iron ore, coal, and limestone from a wooden bridge. The water wheel worked a pair of cylinders that blew air through a tuyere at the bottom of the furnace to fan the fire. (*Design News*, 1976)

Shallow veins of red iron oxide ore had been found locally and for years had been hauled to the Middlebury furnaces by ox-drawn wagons from Springfield, Tallmadge, Northampton, and Copley townships. But when the new furnaces were built in the Cascade valley, a higher-grade ore could be brought in by canal from Zoar. The first boatload of the new raw material arrived on Captain Tallman Beardsley's *Western Star* in October 1832. Once started, cupola furnaces operated continuously, around the clock, for forty weeks, shutting down only in summer, partly because of the intolerable heat generated by the furnace but also to give workers time to tend their farm crops. At night the dazzling bright-yellow glow of raw liquid iron from freshly tapped furnaces could be seen for miles in the industrial valley.

With so much of the ancillary furnace superstructure made of wood—alongside the roaring furnace belching fiery charcoal meteors out of the top—fires were common. The Aetna Furnace between Locks 11 and 12 burned down twice. After it was destroyed by the first fire in 1837, James R. Ford purchased the site and converted it into a foundry, calling it the Akron Manufacturing Company. His facility produced stoves and other cast-iron products. But after the second fire, in 1838, Ford gave up on the hazards of working with molten iron and converted the business into a flour mill, which he called Aetna Mills. Howard & Fenn's furnace at Lock 9 met a similar fate, becoming City Mills. (Ford went on to less risky pursuits, becoming judge of the Court of Common Pleas for Summit County in 1845.) Two new businesses opened in the valley in 1839. Joseph A. Beebe and William E. Wright opened the Center Mill in the building previously occupied by David and Jesse Allen's wool machinery plant at Lock 6, and, downstream at Lock 16, Frank D. Parmelee opened a large tannery on the east side of the canal.

The proliferation of gristmills attracted another Middlebury deserter to the valley to provide a much-needed service. O. H. Cleveland moved his wife and three children to Cascade in 1833 and built the first of many grain warehouses along the canal. In 1840, William B. Mitchell and Judge Leicester King opened the finest flouring mill yet built;

Howard Street at Market, 1858. The Aetna Mill is visible in the background. (University of Akron Archives)

the Cascade Mill opened at Lock 14 on North Street (in the heart of today's park between North Street and the lower trestle). Mitchell made it known that they had spent $8,000 on machinery alone.

Akron's industrial valley was growing. Writing in his diary aboard a canal boat in 1834, Austria's Prince Alexander Philip Maximilian was impressed: "Where the canal expands into a kind of small lake is Akron, a considerable town in a remarkable situation. It already has a considerable trade, many neat wooden houses, stores, manufacturers, an iron foundry, and an establishment where, by means of a wheel, bedsteads and other articles of furniture are turned." By the end of its first decade, the Cascade Race was powering five iron furnaces, several additional flour mills, a woolen mill, a furniture factory, and Payne's distillery, with the same water flowing out of one factory and into the next one—and all of them powered by gravity.

. . .

The baking of bread is much older than the smelting of iron. Grinding grain into flour goes back to the Stone Age: crushing it between rocks or pounding it in a mortar. The first millstones were used in a quern, a primitive mill in which the grain was placed on a flat, circular stone and ground by manually turning another millstone on top of it. Attached to the top stone was a handle that could be worked back and forth or pushed all the way around. Lengthening the handle made it possible for the upper millstone to be turned by a harnessed animal.

It was the Greeks who began to use waterpower to turn millstones in about 450 B.C. The Romans introduced wooden gears to connect several sets of millstones to a single waterwheel, and windmills became common in Europe after the Crusades (probably introduced from Asia Minor). By the nineteenth century, milling had become much more sophisticated. Millstones were no longer just flat, heavy, stone disks. The ones used in gristmills in the Cascade valley were approximately 4 feet in diameter and about a foot thick and were made of sandstone quarried in northeast Ohio—or limestone, if they were imported. Each of the pair of stones weighed about three-quarters of a ton. The upper revolving stone, or runner, had a large hole in the

Model of the nineteenth-century Griebling family gristmill. (Model built by the late Carl Griebling. Photo by the author, courtesy of Steve Griebling)

center into which the grain was fed. It was mounted on an iron spider (or rynd) on the end of a rotating shaft. When the mill was properly adjusted, the millstones never touched each other, so the sandstone should not have added much grit to the flour.

Carved into the top surface of the lower (bed) stone, running from the center to the outer edge, was a pattern of slanted radial V-shaped grooves, an invention of the Romans. There were similar furrows engraved onto the bottom surface of the revolving upper (runner) stone, but these were slanted in the opposite direction. When grain was poured into the center hole, or eye, from an oscillating hopper, the furrows in the upper stone intersected with those in the lower bed stone and repeatedly cut and sheared the grain as it made its way from the center hole to the outer circumference of the stones. The pattern of these grooves was sophisticated, typically starting with about twelve or thirteen grooves in the center of the millstone and then dividing into as many as forty-four by the time they reached the outer edge. Moreover, the grooves grew shallower as the grains and flour were gradually shoved outward toward the periphery.

The millstones were completely enclosed by a cylindrical wooden shroud that minimized dust (because it was explosive) and collected the flour. From the shroud, the flour flowed down a chute and into a bolting chest on the floor below. The chest rotated and was tilted so that the sifted flour flowed out the other end. These mechanized sifters were 14 to 18 feet long, and some had several different sized screens along the length of the reel. Some batches of flour were reground to achieve a finer grade. If this operation was carried out on a higher floor, the flour would be conveyed by a wooden screw auger to an elevator, a series of cups on a vertical chain that dumped the product into a second, finer bolting chest. (Very little was wasted: the Cascade Mill sold screenings, the weed seeds separated from the wheat, for chicken feed at 10 cents for a 10-pound bag.)

All of these operations were turned by massive wooden gears, or by a maze of leather belts turning wooden pulleys of various sizes, driven by a main shaft that was connected to the waterwheel, whose relatively slow speed was multiplied by the gears or belts to turn the upper millstone at one or two revolutions per second.

A miller's job was not an easy one. He had to pick up a sack of grain weighing fifty to seventy pounds from the loading door on the second floor of the mill (deposited there by a rope and pulley) and carry it upstairs to the third floor, where he slowly fed the grain into a funnel-shaped hopper mounted above the pair of millstones on the floor below. A mill could grind fifty pounds of wheat in about ten minutes. After ten minutes, then, the miller went back down to get the next sack. Periodically he went downstairs to the first floor to test the flour by working it in his hands, and he then packaged the sieved contents of the bolting chest in bags or barrels. If the flour was too course or too dry or too "cakie," he would adjust the clearance between the millstones. An experienced miller could tell even by the sound of the mill whether his millstones were doing a good job. Every three or four weeks he dressed the furrows in the stones, using a sharp steel tool to reset the keen edges of the corners. This was an exacting job that was sometimes performed by itinerant dressers who traveled from community to community plying their craft. It took years for an understudy to become a good miller, after which he became a highly respected and extremely valuable member of society.

. . .

Although whiskeymaker Hiram Payne paid Crosby $5,850 for his site and the Allen brothers paid $7,000 for theirs, Howard & Fenn paid only $2,300 for their property. This bargain price may have had something to do with Charles Howard marrying Crosby's daughter, which would also explain Crosby naming his town's main thoroughfare Howard Street.

In 1833, Crosby hired surveyor Albert C. Mallison to lay out his town, and the plat was recorded in Ravenna. In *Akron: City at the Summit,* George Knepper describes what happened next: "Surprisingly, Crosby discarded the name Cascade—already attached to the area—and named his town Akron also. Now there were two Akrons abutting one another along the canal. South Akron—centered around the Main and Exchange corner—claimed 443 souls in 1834. North Akron—at the Main and Howard intersection (sometimes called Hall's Corners)—claimed 440. Rivalry became intense" (30).

When it became apparent that Crosby's North Akron had thirteen retail stores, compared to South Akron's nine, South Akron partisans plotted to influence retail commerce. With the connivance of Middlebury, the South Enders erected a sign at the corner of Market Street and Middlebury Road. Pointing down Middlebury Road (now Buchtel Avenue), the sign read "Akron, One Mile." Exceedingly irked, North Enders turned the sign in the middle of the night so it pointed down Market Street to their community. The sign was changed back and forth several times. Guards were posted. Fists flew—so did rocks. (Several injuries were reported.) Finally reason prevailed, and two new signs were erected, one pointing to North Akron and the other to South Akron. Fortunately, a wedge-shaped piece of undeveloped land known as the Gore lay between the villages, and it became a neutral ground, the site of churches and public buildings (including the courthouse) that catered to both communities.

Pennsylvania & Ohio Canal in downtown Akron, ca. 1850. (University of Akron Archives)

In 1836, under an act of the Ohio General Assembly, the communities combined their 1,343 people into the Town of Akron. The peaceful merger followed a brief land boom (mostly in Crosby's North Akron) that accompanied the resurgence of a venture first planned by a group of private investors as early as 1825. Their objective had been to build a new, independent east-west Pennsylvania & Ohio Canal (also called the Cross-Cut Canal) that would connect Akron with the Ohio River near Pittsburgh.

Optimism soon faded, however. The 1837 financial panic in the Western Reserve dampened hopes that the new canal would ever be completed. Worse, the volume of water from Crosby's dam on the Little Cuyahoga River was decreasing significantly, perhaps due to the cutting of trees in the watershed to convert virgin forest into farmland. Property values plummeted. Things looked bleak. But then in 1838 the General Assembly came through with $420,000 for the project, and the State of Pennsylvania later contributed $50,000. Chief canal engineer Colonel Sebried Dodge began pushing construction work at the Akron end. All through the winter of 1838–39, laborers worked for the handsome wage of 50 cents a day—more than had ever been paid for similar work in this locality—and wages were paid in cash.

The 82-mile Pennsylvania & Ohio Canal (67 miles of it in Ohio) was completed in 1840. Coming from the east and running through Cuyahoga Falls, then down the Little Cuyahoga valley (widening part of Crosby's millrace for part of its right-of-way), it turned south, down the center of Akron's Main Street, connecting with the Ohio & Erie in the Lower Basin just below Lock 1 (next to property where Benjamin Franklin Goodrich would locate his company a half-century later).

Instead of permitting water from the Pennsylvania & Ohio to drain into the Ohio & Erie at its terminus, a lock was built on the new canal on Main Street just south of Mill Street. When closed, the lock directed the flow of excess P&O canal water into Crosby's Mill Street millrace, adding to the water coming from the dam on the Little Cuyahoga River. The operation of nine locks, which were built on the new canal north of Old Forge, allowed more water to flow into the Mill Street millrace, thereby increasing the capacity of the Cascade Race.

Akron would now have two canals running parallel to each other a block apart between Market and Exchange. The Pennsylvania & Ohio Canal formally opened on August 4, 1840, when four brightly decorated packets left New Castle, Pennsylvania, with a party of state dignitaries, signaling the start of a gala that would pick up momentum in Youngstown, Warren, Ravenna, and Franklin Mills (now Kent). The prosperity the new canal would engender was anticipated by communities all along the route, which was lined much of the way with cheering crowds. At Cuyahoga Falls after yet another reception on August 6, two more boats carrying an Akron delegation joined the flotilla. And at Old Forge (which was on a short spur off the P&O) the assemblage was met by six freshly painted Akron boats with banners and pendants flying and carrying not only additional dignitaries from Akron but also the Akron Brass Band. The Pennsylvania fleet was thereafter noisily escorted to Akron's Lower Basin.

By the time the fleet reached Akron, where a reception had been prepared at May's Block, another at the new Ohio Exchange, and yet another at the American House, the canal banks were once again lined with cheering throngs along with competing brass bands and loaded cannons. In addition to Pennsylvania's governor David Wittenhouse Porter, the Pennsylvania boats carried a cargo of sherry and Madeira

Empire House hotel at Main and Market, ca. 1850. (CLPA Archives)

wines as well as imported champagne. The ensuing celebration is said
to have virtually paralyzed Akron business for several days.

The new P&O Canal fulfilled its promise. Land values soared. New
buildings also sprang up in South Akron. A swank new three-story
brick hotel called the Ohio Exchange was erected on the southwest
corner of Main and Market by General Duthan Northrup of Medina. For a decade it was the most popular hotel in the Western Reserve, often hosting visiting celebrities whose horses were cared for
in a large livery stable built next door. Before the Ohio Exchange was
completed, Hiram Payne used some of the profits from his distillery
to build another handsome three-story building a block away on the
corner of Howard and West Market. A tribute to its construction, it
became known as the Stone Block. And the intersection of Market
and Howard earned the name Hall's Corners when Philander D. Hall
of Bridgeport, Connecticut, took over the lease of Seth Iredell's Cascade building and opened a large general store. The Hall family operated the store on this spot for the next sixty years.

A block west of Howard Street, Akron's industrial valley continued to grow. In 1845, just four years after arriving in the United States

from Alsace-Lorraine, twenty-seven-year-old John T. Good (probably translated from Johann T. Gut at Ellis Island) opened Akron's first fledgling brewery near Lock 11, south of Aetna Mills. His partnership in the venture was another German immigrant, sixteen-year-old Michael Bittman. Eight years later, Good purchased Bittman's share of the business for $500, and eventually sold a partial interest in the brewery to his cousin Jacob so he could use some of his beer profits to go into the grocery business.

A major customer for Good's product was the taproom at the new Empire House hotel, built at a cost of $38,000 in 1846–47 by William B. Burroughs and Judge Leicester King. Heralded as the most modern hotel in northern Ohio, the fine brick lodging opened on November 20, 1847, hosting a grand ball and banquet in its elegant ballroom. Perched on top of the four-story structure was a cupola tower where a lookout was stationed to watch for approaching canal boats on the P&O. When one hove into sight he rang a bell to signal the hotel staff that guests might be arriving.

Encouraged by Good's success, another German immigrant, forty-five-year-old George J. Renner, purchased a piece of property in 1848 for $50 near a natural spring at Old Forge. Here, he and partner John Brodt built the George J. Renner Brewing Company. Like many other

The Renner Brewery, built in 1848. (Photo by the author, 2007)

businesses at the time, the brewery suffered major fire damage in 1873 but was rebuilt by its new owner, Frederick Oberholtz. After more than a century and a half, the three-story, architecturally elaborate stone structure still stands at 275 North Forge Street in the valley of the Pennsylvania & Ohio Canal. Set into the ornate brick pattern are huge blocks of sandstone sculpted by stonemasons to read in raised letters, "Boiler-House, Bottling Dept." and at the highest level, for all to see, "Geo. J. Renner." It is one the oldest buildings in Akron.

Meanwhile, in 1841, buoyed by his successes, Dr. Eliakim Crosby was planning a much more ambitious venture in Cuyahoga Falls, one he believed would create a millrace with many times the waterpower of the Cascade Race. In the Cuyahoga River Gorge near Prospect Avenue, he planned to build a 20-foot dam on the river. From here a major hydraulic canal would run west 4 miles to what he had laid out as a huge manufacturing center to be called Summit City. The new village would be on the west side of Main Street's North Hill near the foot of today's Uhler Avenue. Crosby's new town would overlook the Little Cuyahoga Valley. Using his own money for his new enterprise, Crosby hired a large gang of laborers at the very attractive wage of $13 a month; however, only $2 of this would be in cash, with the balance to be paid in the form of a credit at Crosby's company store in the Stone Block at Howard and Market.

The project seemed doomed from the start. Two miles of the waterway would have to be cut from solid rock below the overhanging cliff of the Gorge, and sometimes it had to be built up from river level with masonry. It was dangerous, tedious work that took much longer than Crosby had planned. As with his earlier "river" from Middlebury to the Cascade valley, the project had its doubters. The canal had to be dug across ravines and through the Glens, traversing wild, unsettled territory—wild enough that one local wag, suggesting that the land was inhabited solely by woodchucks, dubbed Crosby's project the Chuckery, a name that stuck.

At last, in May 1844, Crosby announced that he would turn on the water on the morning of the 27th. On the appointed day, crowds gathered along the banks of the ditch to watch the event. When word passed that the water was on the way, the crowd downstream in what was to become Summit City waited expectantly. Hours went by. Noon came and went. Finally, at 4:00 P.M., what was left of the stream arrived. Because the water had been seeping into the porous soil, by the time it arrived it was barely a trickle. "Crosby built his Chuckery Race—only to discover that it literally did not hold water. Because of the hard times, he was unable to secure the additional money required to fix the race [lining the banks and bottom with clay as was standard practice on the canals], and his great scheme collapsed. Chagrined and embarrassed by his failure, Crosby soon left Akron for an obscure town in Wisconsin where he spent his last years. [But] his true monument was the vigorous young Akron which he did so much to build" (Knepper, *Akron*, 32).

. . .

In 1851, German immigrant Ferdinand Schumacher arrived in Akron and opened a small toy and "fancy goods" store on Howard Street at West Market. A year later he built a three-story building on Market Street to house a grocery and drugstore, where, in a back room, he first experimented with making oatmeal, a breakfast cereal unknown in the United States but one he remembered fondly from his childhood in Hanover. After getting a favorable reaction from his family, he began making it regularly, providing an occasional sample to his German friends in the neighborhood and, before long, selling it in his store. By 1856 Schumacher was operating a small oatmeal plant and making a few barrels a day. But in 1861, when his friend Erhard Steinbacher, a major in the Quartermaster Corps, persuaded the Union army's quartermaster general to place a "sample" order for a hundred barrels, it changed Schumacher's life. He immediately hired extra workers and, ignoring laws that forbade working on Sundays, he operated his mini-facility around the clock, seven days a week, and managed to meet the delivery date.

The soldiers loved it—especially compared to the cornmeal mush they had been subjected to. Moreover, the product was easy to ship and didn't spoil. Orders poured in. To meet the demand, Schumacher bought modern machinery and built his German Mill at Howard and North Streets in 1862. It was in operation by the middle of 1863.

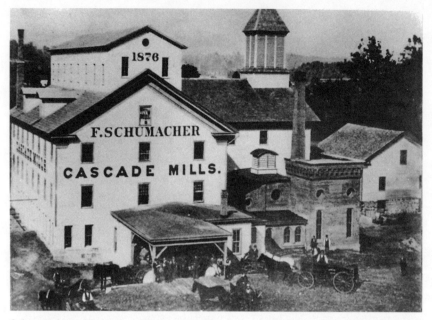

Schumacher's Cascade Mill in 1876 after he refurbished it by adding a thirty-five-foot diameter overshot wheel. (CLPA Archives)

Well established as a supplier by that time, Schumacher was asked by the quartermaster if he could produce pearl barley. He promptly built another new mill on Summit Street near the new railroad depot. Schumacher's Empire Barley Mill was operational by the end of 1863. When his first German Mill in the Cascade valley burned down in 1872, Schumacher built a new German Mill next to his Empire Mill. Later, in 1885, he built his Starch Works on the original German Mill site at Howard and North Streets, a site occupied today by ABTEC, Inc.

By the end of the Civil War, Ferdinand Schumacher was the wealthiest man in Akron. In 1868 he bought the Cascade Mill, the flour mill at Lock 14 built in 1840 by Mitchell and King. However, slowed by the burning of his first German Mill and building its replacement on Summit Street, it took him until 1876 to renovate the Cascade Mill. By the time the Cascade Mill reopened in 1876, Schumacher had installed a state-of-the-art hydraulic system with an overshot iron waterwheel 35 feet in diameter, 10 feet wide, and weighing 37 tons. It was as big as a carnival Ferris wheel, half of it below ground level in the mill pit.

Ruins of Schumacher's overshot wheel (ca. 1912) showing its ninety-six buckets that were filled from a standpipe inside the brick tower. Water came through a closed ceramic pipe from a dam high up in the valley to rise like a siphon to the top of the wheel. (CLPA Archives)

Lock 8, with the canal lined by industries, some of which have added steam power. (University of Akron Archives)

To provide a source of water high enough to feed his overshot wheel from the top, he built a dam high up on the Cascade Race near Lock 11. From the dam, a ceramic pipe 4 feet in diameter carried the water underground down to the mill, rising like a siphon in an 18-foot standpipe, to pour the water over the wheel from a trough 8 feet wide, filling each of its ninety-six buckets, one after the other. Gravity turned the giant wheel three and a half times a minute—one revolution every seventeen seconds—generating 175 horsepower. A tail race carried the water from the bottom of the mill pit to the Little Cuyahoga River in a pair of tunnels. The huge waterwheel turned a wooden pulley 12 feet in diameter inside the mill; attached to the pulley was a leather belt 40 inches wide and 120 feet long. The massive belt drove the main line-shaft inside the mill. Attached to this shaft were twelve pairs of mill-stones, their bolting chests, and all the adjacent mill machinery. The mill was a masterpiece of hydraulic and mechanical engineering.

A table of data submitted to Summit County for the year ending May 31, 1880, covering Schumacher's "Flour and Grist mills" (his German Mill, his Empire Mills, and his Cascade Mills) documents their total capacity as 5,000 bushels of product per day produced by twenty-two pairs of millstones. The capacity of his grain elevators (no doubt at his Empire Mills) was 140,000 bushels.

Unlike some millers, Schumacher did no custom milling. He bought his grain from farmers. His mills operated eleven months a year, and he paid handsome wages for the time: $1.50 per day for an "ordinary laborer" and $2.00 for a "skilled mechanic." He employed a maximum

Schumacher's Cascade Mill, with the Lock 14 basin in the foreground, after Schumacher added his powerhouse with its 125-foot brick chimney to generate steam, which drove a 175-horsepower steam engine to turn additional millstones. (CLPA Archives)

of 100 workers at the three facilities, eighty-eight males (minimum age sixteen) and twelve females (minimum age fifteen), and unlike some contemporary factories that exploited children, he reported zero "children or youth."

Schumacher was the last of the waterpower innovators in the Cascade valley. Other industries had begun to sprout smokestacks. As the October 1856 issue of *Scientific American* warned:

> It has now become a serious question with many manufacturers using waterpower, that their supply of water is becoming more unstable every year as the forests are cleared off. Many streams once flowing with water for the miller are now only water-worn channels. But manufactures have not decreased in our country, thanks to the power of steam. With a plentiful supply of fuel (coal), steam forms a constant trusty power for driving machinery, and a steam factory can be erected independent of rare natural localities like water-falls. Steam factories can be conducted in or near cities and commercial marts.

Moreover, as entrepreneurs in the Cascade valley soon learned, steam is also a much more powerful medium. The increased energy available from steam is dictated by the laws of physics: one ton of water falling one mile releases about the same amount of energy as the burning of one pound of coal.

When Alexander Cummins and Albert Allen purchased Crosby's famous Stone Mill in 1861, they installed new machinery and also supplemented the mill's waterpower with a 125-horsepower steam engine, which ran five of the eleven pairs of millstones. Before long their mill was shipping 300 barrels of flour a day. Their closest competitor was Philo Chamberlain, who purchased the Aetna Mills in 1862. He, too, added a steam engine, boosting his mill's capacity to 200 barrels a day.

When Ferdinand Schumacher finally added steam to the Cascade Mills, he once again did it with state-of-the-art thoroughness. He built a separate powerhouse with a massive boiler and a 125-foot brick chimney, which initially ran a 160-horsepower steam engine. Impressed by the power of the new technology, he added three more boilers, one of which he installed in the main mill building to run a 175-horsepower

Aetna Mills at Lock 12 in 1881, after it added steam power. (CLPA Archives)

engine in the basement (which is why the smokestack on the brick standpipe tower was lengthened).

Then, in 1887, having heard about the discovery of natural gas in Ohio, Schumacher drilled a 500-foot well that produced enough gas to fire the several boilers in his Cascade Mill (which he valued as a $10,000 savings on coal). Ever the entrepreneur, he then resumed drilling and at 1,000 feet broke into a source of higher-pressure gas that he piped to other F. Schumacher Milling Company mills. He may also have sold some of it to other industries in the valley, increasing the value of his well to $25,000, an amount that translates into more than half a million of today's dollars.

Using both steam and waterpower, by 1892 Schumacher's Cascade Mill was turning eighteen pairs of millstones, eight bolting chests, and other mill accessories. The lamps for his night shift (which had been fueled by lard or, later, kerosene) were replaced with electric lights powered by his own steam-driven dynamo.

The age of steam had arrived in Akron. One company proudly called itself the Akron Steam Forge Company. Maps in Summit County's 1874 *Atlas* show a number of new industries whose locations make it apparent that their machinery could not have been driven by water-power. In the Cascade valley these included two wood-planing mills, a flour mill, two varnish companies, and a tannery. When Benjamin Franklin Goodrich moved his rubber company from Melrose, New York, to the bank of the Ohio Canal at Lock 1 in 1870, he used the heat available from steam to cure his rubber products and he used canal water to cool the steel rolls of his rubber mills. And he could ship his products on the adjacent canal. (Goodrich's initial product was fire hose, which his company had made in New York. It was an item that found a ready market in Akron, with its history of major fires, especially in the town's early years. During the 1850s, scores of frame buildings in the business section went up in smoke, and on November 1, 1853, a single fire in the industrial valley consumed three cast-iron stove factories, the town's largest blast furnace, two flour mills, the planing mill, and a barrel factory. Some of those fires were undoubtedly set, since, in that decade alone, four firebugs were convicted and sent to prison.)

Steam invaded the valley in a metaphorical way in 1879 when the Valley Line began constructing a railroad bridge over the canal 40 feet above Lock 13. Looking like it was constructed out of telephone poles, a 300-foot-long wooden trestle marked the beginning of the end of

Behind the ruins of the Cascade Mill waterwheel is the first Valley Line railroad trestle in the background. This first (lower) trestle was built of wood in 1879. (CLPA Archives)

G 4484 Looking down the Canal, Akron, O.

The first high trestle was built of steel by the Pittsburgh, Akron & Western Railroad in 1889–90. (Ruth Kleinfelter)

Ohio's canal era. The city had been served since 1852 by a locally financed spur rail line that had built a small wooden station at Mill and Summit Streets, but this crude viaduct across the Cascade Race and the Ohio Canal seemed like a direct assault. It was on January 28, 1880, during a season in which the canals in the northern part of the state were usually frozen, that the first through train crossed the new bridge. Leaving Cleveland at 9:30 A.M., it arrived in Canton at 1:00 P.M. On the return trip it made the 60-mile run in exactly two hours, blowing away the 4-mile-per-hour pace of the mule-drawn canal boats. Regular passenger and freight traffic between the towns began February 2.

Ten years later the Pittsburgh, Akron & Western Railroad built a slim, lofty steel bridge over Lock 11 that was almost three times as long. The ethereal structure soared 70 feet over the canal. The stone foundations for its steel towers can still be seen from the canal towpath. Both trestles were replaced early in the twentieth century.

The railroads actually bolstered commerce in the valley. In 1865, after hearing about the petroleum-shipping center in Oil City, Pennsylvania, that sprung up after E. L. Drake's discovery in nearby Titusville, brewer John T. Good began importing tank cars of crude oil to

A Valley Line steam locomotive in 1910. (CLPA Archives)

make kerosene in a new plant he built on Furnace Street. Kerosene was vastly cheaper (if more explosive) than whale oil, and by 1872 Good was refining 250 barrels a day, and he became one of the first exporters of lamp oil to Europe.

. . .

Meanwhile, the downtown portion of the city adjacent to the industrial valley had grown substantially. By 1870 the population of Akron exceeded 10,000, and people were finding the time and money for entertainment. They could afford to have fun. It was the year that Dr. James Peterson built his Ice Palace at the bottom of the Market Street hill, near the bridge over the canal, by grading a shallow pool flooded by the canal, 161 feet long by 62 feet wide, letting nature take its course at what he called "the coldest place in Akron." To light (and to glorify) his ice rink, Peterson surrounded it with five circles of gas burners, with twenty-five flaming torches in each circle. And on January 7, the night the Ice Palace opened, music was provided by Marple's Band and Keating's Orchestra. As the *Summit County Beacon* reported, "Some skaters danced the polka and the schottische [while others] skated gracefully over the flint-like ice as the men linked arm in arm with their favorite companions, laughing and singing."

Two years earlier Julius Sumner had built the forty-eight-room Sumner House hotel on the southeast corner of Howard and Federal Streets (then called Tallmadge). In addition, as what he hoped would be a mark of gentrification, he built a single-story frame building with a small stage at one end. The bare wood floor was covered with folding chairs, which could be removed for dances. He had the hubris to call it the Sumner Opera House. But his Opera House was eclipsed in 1871 with the completion of the architecturally grand Academy of Music at Main and Market. Built of brick and sculptured stone, the lavish four-story theater opened with fanfare on Monday, June 12, with a production of *Lady Audley's Secret,* a play that ran for two nights. It was followed on Wednesday evening by *Leah the Forsaken, East Lynn* on Thursday night, *Hunchback* on Friday, and, finishing out the week, Shakespeare's *Macbeth* on Saturday. In reviewing the opening performance, the *Akron City Times* declared the Academy of Music was "the neatest and handsomest place of public amusement in the country."

. . .

Although the Ohio & Erie Canal continued to haul substantial freight, the Pennsylvania & Ohio encountered a direct onslaught by the Cleveland & Mahoning Railroad, which ran between Cleveland and Youngstown. It was in their Youngstown office that the railroad executives witnessed the hundreds of tons of iron ore arriving daily in the steel city by canal boat. Unable to compete with the economics of transporting eighty tons of ore by three mules in tandem when speed didn't count, the railroad embarked on a plan to put the canal out of business and it began buying up P&O stock until it had acquired a controlling interest—after which, as the majority stockholder, the road insisted on boosting canal toll rates. The incessant rate hikes imposed by the railroad eventually dropped toll receipts on the canal from $8,790 in 1856 to $772 by 1862, at which time the connivers persuaded the State of Ohio to sell its $420,000 block of stock to "the highest bidder." Since Cleveland & Mahoning was the only bidder, the railroad acquired the state's stock for $35,000, after which the new owner abandoned the canal east of Ravenna. Before long, overgrown with water plants, the canal turned into a mosquito breeding ground.

The P&O in north Akron escaped such infestation since the canal water north of Mill Street was kept moving by the continued input from Crosby's venerable hydraulic canal from his Middlebury dam. But south of the lock at Mill Street and all the way to Exchange Street, the canal became a long, algae-covered, stinking pond. A movement arose to condemn the canal as a public nuisance. But this would have shut off the Cascade Race—a move the mill owners in the valley wouldn't stand for. The impasse lasted for a decade. As Karl Grismer tells the story,

Then came the night of Monday, December 8, 1873. A cold winter rain was falling. The single oil lamp which stood at Main and Exchange could barely be seen half a block away. Constable James McAllister stepped out of Steese's Hotel on the northwest corner of the intersection, looked around, shivered, and went back inside. The town clock on the German Reformed Church up on Broadway struck the hour of midnight.

Suddenly, apparently from all directions, came groups of men numbering almost a hundred. With them came a dozen teams [of horses]. The men and teams headed for a sand bank a little west of the Ohio Canal. (233)

For more than an hour, the conspirators hauled wagonloads of sand to the middle of the wooden bridge over the Pennsylvania & Ohio Canal at Exchange Street, filling the canal to the water level. Then, Grismer continues,

A small group got carried away, and walked north to Middlebury Street [Buchtel Avenue], where they cut the canal bank.

With a roar that could be heard for blocks, the water gushed into the flats below, causing much damage at Christy's Tannery and at John Baker's Cigar Box Manufactory, and wrecking Lock 4 on the Ohio Canal. All of the water drained from the P&O between Exchange Street and the lock at Mill Street. The canal boat *Armstrong* was left stranded near Center Street. Their mission accomplished, the workmen dispersed. So did the crowd that had gathered. The cold rain kept falling. Constable McAllister, who had again emerged from the warm hotel and witnessed the proceedings from a distance, did nothing, and went back to the fireside. (234)

Prosecutorial action against the perpetrators became stymied in the courts, mostly by lawyers of prominent citizens who secretly applauded the move. Years went by. While the hearings dragged on, the City Council eventually ordered the canal to be filled in between Mill and Exchange—an action that wasn't finally accomplished until 1884.

. . .

Meanwhile, signs of technological modernization were emerging. In 1877, B. F. Goodrich had a telephone line strung from his home on Water Street to his rubber factory on the Ohio Canal, a prestigious move soon imitated by other industrialists. By 1880 the Akron Telephone Company had strung 160 miles of wire on 200 poles and was serving 160 subscribers. Photos taken during this decade instantly date themselves with their forest of telephone poles, each having as many as a dozen crossbars studded with glass insulators.

In 1881 the Akron Waterworks began operation with five drilled wells and a pumping station, finally solving the inadequacies (especially for firefighting) of private wells, rainwater cisterns, and private commercial suppliers, among them the Akron Cold Spring Company, which gave Aqueduct Street its name. Two years later steel rails were laid on Howard and Main Streets by the Akron Street Railway and Herdic Company. By 1887 the horse-drawn Herdic Line had been extended to Lakeside Park (which later became Summit Beach) on the east side of Summit Lake. A year later, in October 1888, the Akron Street Railway was electrified. The sprightly new four-wheeled trolleys on Howard Street were double-ended, rolling back and forth on a single set of tracks. The motorman and conductor switched places at each end of the line and swung the trolley pole around before retracing the route.

Karl Grismer recounts the adventures that went along with being a passenger on John Seiberling's Howard Street line after it was extended up North Hill:

In 1888 the horse-drawn Herdic Line steetcars were replaced by electric trolleys, whose power was generated in the valley near Lock 10. (University of Akron Archives)

At times when the power was weak, heavily loaded cars were stalled on the hill, and not until years later could two cars go up the hill at the same time, even when lightly loaded. During rush hours, cars had to line up in the valley and await their turn.

When cars had to stop while going up the hill, passengers held their breath. They had reason to be apprehensive. More then once the brakes failed to hold and the cars shot madly backward, lurching from side to side, with the m ɔto ·m.ɪn frantically clanging his bell. Once, one of these runaway cars crashed into another car in the valley. Old timers recall one person was killed and two seriously injured. (281)

The direct current in the trolley wires that served the city's electric streetcars was generated by a steam-driven dynamo installed in a new brick building erected near Lock 10 next to King Varnish, which had been established in 1882 by David L. King at Beech and Canal Streets (near the north end of today's Park behind the Interbelt Nite Club). By the turn of the century this DC power plant, owned by Northern Ohio Traction Company, was also selling electricity to businesses in downtown Akron. And in 1902, having purchased its rivals, temporarily securing a monopoly on providing Akron's electricity, the name of the company was changed to Northern Ohio Traction & Light. But by 1927 municipal power generation had been picked up by several larger electric utilities, including the London & Power Company and the Pennsylvania-Ohio Power & Light Company, which had the capacity to serve more of the community. So, putting their steam boilers back to work, the company became the Akron Steam Heating Company. Its six conveyor-fed boilers were vented by its three tall, trademark smokestacks. For the next forty years Northern Ohio Traction & Light would provide heat to 344 customers in downtown Akron through 13.7 miles of steam lines. When the Great Depression struck the nation in 1929, Akron Steam Heating became one of five businesses, including the above two power companies, that merged to become the Ohio Edison Company, which explains why the site survived as an Ohio Edison transformer station until the long-idle steam plant was torn down in 2006 (because its steam pipes had been insulated with asbestos).

. . .

By the mid-1880s Ferdinand Schumacher had acquired a dozen competitors who were making oatmeal, or rolled oats. In making oatmeal, the seed grains were partially cooked or steamed before being cracked open between a pair of iron rolls. Schumacher's eight-story Jumbo Mills on Broadway (now Quaker Square) was the largest mill in the world. Here he invented (but never patented) pneumatic conveying, whereby he blew grain from his silos on Broadway through underground pipes down to a second plant on the canal at Lock 5.

But before dawn on March 6, 1886, Schumacher's fortunes were disastrously changed when a dust explosion occurred in one of the Jumbo Mills grain-drying houses. Within minutes the structure was ablaze. The fire spread rapidly, engulfing dozens of buildings, including grain elevators. Akron's twelve-man fire department was overwhelmed despite the valiant reinforcement efforts of volunteers from as far away as Kent and Cleveland, who arrived by special trains. The fire raged for two days, consuming the entire Jumbo Mills complex and resulting in a loss of $600,000 (equivalent to more than $10 million today).

Frugal, independent, and obstinate, Schumacher carried no insurance. His imprudence cost him dearly and ultimately forced him to join his competitors in a cartel. The new American Cereal Company, established in 1888, merged all of Schumacher's properties (including the Cascade Mills) with those of the Akron Milling Company and several others. But because his name was so closely associated with the product, and because he was a major stockholder in the new enterprise, he was appointed president, a job for which the admitted "stubborn Dutchman" was not well suited, especially when it came to marketing breakfast cereal. He believed, for example, that advertising was utterly wasteful. And he was convinced that oatmeal should be sold in fifty-pound bags. As president, he forced the ouster of executives who disagreed with his ideas. His very capable production manager eventually resigned in protest.

Schumacher hated losing his independence. But since he was still one of the wealthiest men in Akron, he had been borrowing heavily against his remaining assets to purchase a majority interest in American Cereal Company stock. His venture was badly timed, however, since a lengthy financial panic was beginning to take hold of the nation. Defaulting on his ill-timed loans drove him into bankruptcy, and in 1896 the Probate Court of Summit County forced him to assign all of his assets (listed as a staggering $2.4 million) to a receiver. In 1898 he lost his stock in the American Cereal Company, which was purchased in 1901 by a new cereal combine called the Quaker Oats Company. Undaunted, he formed a new partnership with his sons, Adolph and Lewis, and founded the Schumacher Cereal Mills in Iowa City, Iowa. (Thus, contrary to what has become a popular myth, Schumacher was not the founder of Quaker Oats. He was never associated with the company.)

In Akron's industrial valley, early on Sunday, March 7, 1904, the Cascade Mill burned. According to a July 21, 1925, article in the *Akron Beacon Journal,* "C. H. Wheeler was the owner at the date of the fire, which is listed on the Fire Department's books as being of incendiary origin, although no one was ever arrested in connection with the blaze."

Ferdinand Schumacher died at his home on East Market Street at the age of eighty-six on April 15, 1908, proud to note that all of his debts had been paid off—and with compound interest. In announcing his passing, the *Summit County Beacon* reminisced on April 15, 1908, that "the poor German immigrant dies little better off than when he came to Akron; yet in his life here he has been a tower of strength, a factor that will always make his name respected and revered by all familiar with the city's history."

. . .

By the 1880s the composition of the industries in the canal valley had changed significantly. Many had closed or had moved to other locations. But Dr. Goodrich's rubber company at Lock 1 had emerged as Akron's largest employer. After early years of struggle, the company's product line had diversified to include (solid) rubber tires for buggies, which tapped an expanding market. The company's founder lived long enough to see his enterprise pass $500,000 in sales, but he was denied the opportunity to participate in his company's later triumph. After suffering from tuberculosis for many years, Benjamin Franklin Goodrich moved to Colorado in 1888 for that state's purportedly therapeutic climate, but he died there later that year.

The year 1888 also saw Scottish veterinarian John Boyd Dunlop's invention of the pneumatic tire for bicycles, and the B. F. Goodrich Company took a license on it in 1889, just as the bicycle craze was beginning to sweep the nation. On the high-wheeler bikes of the day, riders sat directly over the axle of the 5-foot-diameter wheel, and the very welcome air-filled tire was the only cushioning they had when bumping along on the cobblestone (or unpaved) streets of the time. The air-filled tire turned out to be an enormous boon to the bicycle industry. By 1899 there were 312 bicycle factories in the nation, making a million bikes a year. And the replacement market for the new air-filled tires was substantial because bicycles shared the road with horses, which often left horseshoe nails in their wake.

But at the turn of the century, a new form of personal transportation was unveiled. The New York Auto Show, inaugurated at Madison Square Garden in 1900, displayed thirty-four models of the 4,192 motor vehicles produced that year. Nineteen of the models were driven by internal combustion engines fueled by gasoline, seven by steam, six by electricity, and two by a reassuring combination of gas and electricity.

An early Jackson auto with white pneumatic tires, ca. 1910. (Edgar F. Gieck)

All of them, however, ran on rubber tires—some on solids, others on pneumatics—and B. F. Goodrich, having already mastered the technology for making both, had a display in the balcony. Within a decade, auto production would grow to more than 200,000 units annually as the number of manufacturers increased geometrically.

The U.S. Census of 1890 showed that there were ninety-four rubber plants in the United States at the time. Akron had just one, and Goodrich was listed among the also-rans. But, inspired by Goodrich's record, a rubber boom erupted in the city in the 1890s. Akron's second rubber manufacturer was started by three owners of a drugstore who pooled their savings in 1892 to found the Miller Rubber Company. Diamond Rubber was next, established in 1894, and followed by the Akron India Rubber Company in 1895. Then, in 1898, the Seiberling brothers founded what would become the world's largest rubber company, calling it Goodyear—ostensibly to honor the inventor of vulcanization but actually to have a name that sounded like the highly successful Goodrich. In Chicago, Harvey Firestone, a buggy tire salesman who also operated a service facility, saw the potential offered by the automobile, and he returned to Ohio in 1900 to estab-lish the company that bears his name.

Other names that would emerge in greater Akron include Kelly-Springfield, the Faultless Rubber Company, Motz Clincher Tire & Rubber Company, Stein Double Cushion Tire Company, the Union Rubber Company, Rubber Products Company, Electric Products Company, the Portage Rubber Company, Falls Rubber Company, and Marathon Tire & Rubber Company. By 1905 there were more people employed in the rubber industry in Akron than in any other city in the nation—a statistic that would hold for a century. (General Tire did not join the list until 1915, when William O'Neil sold his family's department store to the May Company.)

The rubber industry returned to the Cascade valley in 1904 when James A. Swinehart built the Swinehart Clincher Tire & Rubber company on the site of Schumacher's first German Mill at 21 West North Street to produce a solid-rubber tire design on which he had

An early pneumatic tire-manufacturing line in Akron. (University of Akron Ar-chives)

been awarded more than twenty patents. Basically, his unique design kept the tire from coming off the wheel when the car made a sharp turn. By 1911 Swinehart's factory ranked sixth among Akron's rubber companies, and by 1916 he was making 500 tires a day and achieving $1.6 million in sales. But when the Great Depression of 1929 struck the nation, the company filed for bankruptcy. (The three-story brick structure has been occupied since 1985 by ABTEC, Inc., a dealer in recycled commercial and industrial equipment.)

In 1912 the American Tire Company was built on the site of Aetna Mills between Locks 11 and 12, and a major expansion followed in 1916. By 1920 the company ran three shifts, turning out 600 tires a day and posting annual sales of $5 million. But like many other Akron companies, American Tire filed for bankruptcy in 1929. The buildings remained idle until 1935, when Floyd Snyder founded the Ace Rubber Company. He was able to use American Tire's rubber-mixing equipment, which had remained in the building since the company's demise. In continuous operation since 1935, and now under the ownership of Charles Garro, Ace Rubber makes custom decorative rubber flooring.

. . .

By the turn of the century, freight traffic on the canal between Akron and Cleveland had dwindled to the coal boats from Clinton and Navarre that regularly hauled fuel for Cleveland's lake steamers. Nearly all of the locks leaked because much of the mortar between the lock stones had washed out. The leakage might have been avoidable if early settler Jonathan Hale (of Hale Farm) had known more about Ohio geology when he arrived in what was then Portage County in 1810. Hale had been a bricklayer in Glastonbury, Connecticut, and he knew how to make mortar. So in 1825 Hale solicited and received a contract to make the mortar for the forty-four locks between Akron and Cleveland. Lime for mortar was made by "burning" limestone over a bed of glowing charcoal, driving off carbon dioxide from the calcium carbonate rock and leaving calcium oxide, or quicklime, behind. When mixed with water, this becomes slaked lime, a pasty calcium hydroxide mixture used to fasten bricks, or lock stones, together. After drying, the mortar gradually picks up carbon dioxide from the air, reforming calcium carbonate, and the bonding agent becomes nearly as strong as the original limestone. But there is very little limestone in northeast Ohio, so Hale apparently used any kind of rock that looked promising.

Because keeping the canal adequately filled with water had become a constant problem, the state decided to do something about it in an effort to encourage more canal traffic, including for recreational use. So in 1906 the state awarded a major contract to the Daley Brothers' Construction Company to waterproof all the locks in this part of Ohio, a project that took two years to complete and that included refurbishing the wooden gates.

Instead of caulking the lock stones with new quicklime mortar, which would have been labor-intensive, requiring hundreds of bricklayers, the Daley Brothers elected to rebuild most of the locks with concrete. To preserve the 15-foot width of locks, the workmen chipped back the lock walls about 6 inches and filled the space with a mixture of Portland cement and sand (occasionally adding salvaged lock stones). The resulting concrete face into which the Daley Brothers proudly cast their names (together with their 1906–7 dates of completion) is visible on the walls of several of the Cascade Locks.

But six years later the construction company's efforts would be devastated. March 1913 brought Ohio's entire canal system to an abrupt end. After a winter of record snowfall, spring rains had been abnormally heavy throughout the state. On Sunday morning, March 23, a torrential downpour began and continued for days. The Little Cuyahoga River was so out of its banks that houses were floating away in east Akron. At 9:00 Monday morning, having already quenched the fires in Goodyear's powerhouse, it washed out the Howard Street Bridge.

As the level of the Portage Lakes reservoirs continued to rise, many of the fashionable summer homes lining their shores were inundated. Then, at midnight on Monday, when the storm was at its height, the dam on the East Reservoir gave way (some believe it was dynamited), releasing a massive volume of impounded water into Long Lake, and from there it poured into the canal opposite Young's Tavern on Manchester Road. Here the torrent divided, part of it going south toward Barberton and the rest rushing north through Akron, sometimes roaring several feet over the tops of the lock gates. The water poured into

Houses floated away on the Little Cuyahoga River during the 1913 flood. (University of Akron Archives)

the basements of scores of warehouses and retail stores along the canal, and it drowned the boilers of the Northern Ohio Traction & Light power plant at Lock 10, extinguishing the lights in downtown Akron.

On Tuesday morning, when he saw what was happening, John Henry Vance, a B.F. Goodrich engineer who was former chairman of the Waterways Commission in Akron, recruited an army of workers from the Goodrich plant to fill burlap sacks, feed bags, and flour sacks from wagonloads of dirt that had been brought in. The men built their levee in a continuous downpour of rain. Vance related his story to this writer in an interview in 1951:

By 9:00 P.M. on Tuesday the makeshift levee began to crumble, and the wall of water flowing over the tops of the gates threatened to engulf downtown Akron, including the boilers in the Goodrich plant, which bordered the canal. Vance telegraphed the state offices in Columbus and was given executive authority in the emergency. He called his friend Tom McShaffrey, an Akron contractor who knew of a nearby construction site where some dynamite was stored. By the light of a lantern, they located the dynamite chest, broke open the lock, and removed six sticks, taking along a length of pipe lying nearby. At Lock 1 they tied the dynamite, along with a concrete block for added weight, to one end of the pipe. After putting an electric cap into one of the sticks, Vance plunged the business end of the pipe into the depths at the base of the lock and rolled over the levee, signaling McShaffrey to fire the charge.

A geyser of water shot into the night air, illuminated by the flash at its source, and millions of tons of unleashed water—the entire Summit Level volume—crashed through all of the remaining gates of the Cascade Locks below, ending the canal in Akron for all time.

Dawn on Wednesday brought with it a cold wave and an end to the

After the 1913 flood, the lower railroad bridge was replaced by a steel trestle supported on concrete arches. (CLPA Archives)

rain. A total of 9.6 inches of rain had fallen in Akron. Across the state, 752 lives had been lost, and property damage mounted into the hundreds of millions. Although portions of the canal system would be restored for industrial water supply (used primarily by Firestone and Goodrich), commercial canal traffic came to an end on March 24, 1913.

The *Akron Beacon Journal* had the biggest story since its founding in 1839 (as the *Beacon*). Its photographers had captured dramatic images of the devastation—houses floating on the Little Cuyahoga River, shattered lock gates, the remains of businesses laid waste by the flood—yet with Akron's power plant flooded at Lock 10, the newspaper was paralyzed. But with ingenuity typical of Akron entrepreneurs, the newspapermen brought in a motorcycle and, attaching a belt to the rear wheel, managed to drive a small dynamo, generating enough current to get one Linotype machine operating. Putting together an abbreviated edition, they took the page makeups of set type to the Werner Printing Company, an east Akron book publisher at Perkins and Union Streets that had its own power plant, permitting the *Beacon Journal* to go to press. The abbreviated, magazine-size newspaper described "the most strenuous 12 hours in Akron's history" under the three-tiered headline:

FIVE LIVES LOST; 500 HOMELESS;
MILLIONS OF DAMAGE; AS FLOOD
SWEEPS OVER CUYAHOGA VALLEY

. . .

There is only one nineteenth-century commercial structure left in the Cascade valley. It is the general store at Lock 15 that served both the Cascade community and passing canal boats. It was opened in about 1853 by thirty-year-old Frederick Mustill (his father, Joseph, who lived in the house next door, may have operated a business on the site earlier). And it was, indeed, a general store. Ledger entries of the day included pork, ham, beef, corned beef, beefsteak, mutton, fish, cheese, sugar, molasses, whiskey, beer, brandy, cider, coffee, tea, wheat, corn, oats, hay, apples, turnips, cabbage, pumpkins, onions, potatoes, cucumbers, tobacco, nails, candles, oil, soap, scythes, and matches. A flyer Mustill

The Mustill Store, ca. 1860. (CLPA Archives)

printed in late 1853 advertises a number of newly imported hardware items: "Washboards, Combs, Lanterns, Pins, Shoe Brushes, Window Glass, Shot, Starch, [clay] Pipes, Textiles, Crocks & Flasks, Rope, Items of Clothing." And two condiments were added to the list of sundries: "Pepper Sauce and Saleratus [baking soda]." These goods were probably brought in by canal and unloaded while the boats were in the lock in front of the store. An entry for a sale of provisions to a Mr. Rose on November 22, 1853, lists "whiskey, lard, pork, vinegar, sugar, salt, butter, rice, 1 mop, 1 broom, crackers, tea, starch, pipes, flour, tallow, pork & beans, pepper sauce," and a "hoghead of beer."

The store's location was perfect for a commercial venture. Coming from Cleveland, the towpath crossed over the canal from the east side to the west on a wooden bridge in front of the store. As an added inducement for the boatmen to tarry, the store provided a watering trough, or "swilling place," for the mules while the boats negotiated the lock, giving passengers and crew time to buy refreshments (beer, whiskey, brandy, coffee, and tea offered for sale). And since the stop was one

The Mustill Store and Lock 15, after the lock was restored by the Daley Brothers. The towpath crossed the canal in front of the store. On the right are early power and telephone lines. (CLPA Archives)

day out of Cleveland, with thirty-nine locks negotiated to get this far, it gave the boat's cook an opportunity to buy fresh fruit and vegetables.

Frederick Mustill and his wife, Emma, lived next door in what is still called the Mustill House, the residence that had belonged to Fred's father, Joseph Mustill, who moved to a farm in 1851. The couple had a two-year-old daughter at the time and a son, Frederick William, who was born in March 1853. Fred Mustill operated the store for thirty-five years, during which time he and Emma had four more children, only two of whom lived to adulthood. By 1875 sons Edwin and Franklin were serving as clerks in their father's store. Ed went on to win local fame as a piccolo player and leader of Mustill's Orchestra.

In 1880 Frederick Mustill was listed in the *City Directory* as a "Dealer in Ice." This was, of course, before the age of refrigeration, and harvesting ice from the frozen canal in winter had become common. The sawed blocks were stored in sawdust and straw, which helped some of the ice last well into summer. To increase their harvest, some entrepreneurs dug adjacent ice ponds, which were flooded by canal water. The Mustill ice was probably stored in the back of the store in the well-insulated, stone-walled addition to the building, which may have been part of a structure erected by Joseph Mustill before the wood-frame store was built by his son.

By 1888 the family had moved to a home on North Walnut Street, where Fred Mustill died two years later, after which Emma returned to the Mustill House with son Frank. Frank left when he married in 1904, and then granddaughter Emma Louise Hardy and her husband, John, moved in with grandmother Emma until her death in 1911. In a 1907 photograph of Lock 15 after its restoration by the Daley Brothers, the aging Mustill Store appears to still be in fairly good condition. But a few years later the porch and its roof with six supporting columns were washed away.

According to city records, ownership of the store remained in the Mustill family until 1940, but it became a residence after 1903 and saw a succession of tenants. In 1955 both the store and the adjacent house were purchased by Pete and Julia Ramnytz, who lived in the Mustill House until 1989. Ramnytz used the store as a personal warehouse for electric motors, other electrical and mechanical hardware items, a large collection of old newspapers, and other personal treasures.

Then in 1987, University of Akron biology professor Walter Sheppe, an avocational historian and photographer, learned that Pete Ramnytz wanted to move to Florida and was looking for a buyer for the house and store. Recognizing that these were two of the oldest structures in Akron, Sheppe took the news to Virginia Wojno (now Wojno-Forney), president of Akron's Progress Through Preservation group. Intrigued by the possibilities, Wojno put together an ancillary "Save the Mustill Store Committee," which tried to raise the modest sum of $24,000 to purchase the two run-down properties. Finally, in desperation, the committee members agreed to personally invest $5,000 each in the project. "When Jim Alkire, Akron's planning director, saw that we were serious," Wojno said, "he arranged for the city to purchase the properties, and then asked me, 'Okay, you've got your property. Now what are you going to do with it?'"

The restored Mustill Store was opened as a museum in July 2000. (CLPA Archives)

Wojno accepted the challenge, making a commitment that would reshape her life. She began by forming the nonprofit Cascade Locks Park Association. The name had been suggested by Congressman John Seiberling, a personal friend and mentor who had earlier fathered the Cuyahoga Valley National Recreation Area, now the Cuyahoga Valley National Park. Launching her new organization with a luncheon on March 6, 1989, at the Akron City Club, Wojno invited more than two dozen candidates, many of whom expressed interest. Using an administrative tool familiar to successful movers and shakers of volunteer organizations, she appointed a number of committee chairmen, and she persuaded Dr. Arlyn Melcher of Kent State University to be the new association's first president.

The product of the cooperative effort was the establishment of the Cascade Locks Park under a partnership between the City of Akron and Metro Parks, Serving Summit County—a resource that would be developed by the Cascade Locks Park Association and operated by Metro Parks, Serving Summit County. The crown jewel of the new park was to be the Mustill Store. But after the Ramnytzs moved out of the adjacent house, the pair of unpainted, boarded-up structures isolated in the woods looked like they had been abandoned.

The Akron Junior Chamber of Commerce offered to help. They put new temporary siding on the store to improve its appearance, and one of the organization's officers, a University of Akron professor of marketing, arranged for one of his students to become a token-rent tenant who would live in the Mustill House.

But then the young man suddenly moved out (to become a Chippendale dancer!). So Professor Doug Hausknecht and his two dogs made the unique personal sacrifice of moving into the house. Dr. Hausknecht lived in the disintegrating structure for nearly a year, surviving the winter of 1992–93. He vividly remembers both sunlight and winter winds streaming in through the cracks in his second floor bedroom walls, while downstairs his dogs' water dish froze to the floor. Hausknecht was replaced the following summer by a couple sympathetic to the project. They lived in the house for several years, adding drywall, plaster, and carpet to make it more livable.

Meanwhile, the Cascade Locks Park Association had been raising funds for the renovation of both the store and the house and had begun soliciting bids. After a century and a half of decay, these buildings were ready for the care and attention of professionals. To the delight of the CLPA Building Committee, John Debo, the new superintendent of the Cuyahoga Valley National Recreation Area, was interested in the project. In his career with the National Park Service, Debo had supervised historic restorations. He took on the responsibility of coordinating all phases of the Mustill project, in close cooperation with the CLPA Building Committee, which met with his representatives weekly. By 2000 (the same year that John Debo's Cuyahoga Valley National Recreation Area became the Cuyahoga Valley National Park), the Mustill Store and the adjacent Mustill House were restored to vintage condition.

. . .

The store opened to the public in July 2000. Its original Greek Revival front bore signs offering "Groceries & Provisions" and the adjoining "Meat Market." The restored interior, with its cast-iron stove, retail counters, and even the original wooden chute that dispensed grain from the second floor to fill sacks in the service area, is now a museum decorated with scores of antique photographs, vintage furniture, and nineteenth-century hardware. The store's second floor houses the offices of the Cascade Locks Park Association.

Since Bridge Garvin became its executive director in 2001, the CLPA has grown from 150 members to 510 today, and the Cascade Locks Park has come alive with activities. The store and its museum have become tourist attractions frequently visited by hikers and bicyclists on the canal towpath trail. The store is hosted by CLPA volunteers, some of whom have been trained as docents to lead visitor tours through the park.

On the south side of North Street, across from the Mustill Store and Mustill House, are the buried ruins of Schumacher's Cascade Mill. A two-year archaeological dig, completed in 2004 in cooperation with the University of Akron's Department of Anthropology, Archaeology, and Classical Studies, was successful in uncovering the foundation of the Cascade Mill's barrel house and that of the powerhouse as well as in identifying an assortment of artifacts buried when the basin at Lock 14 was filled in during the early twentieth century to erect the Ohio Edison high-voltage tower in the park.

The Cascade Locks Park Association has a Howard Street Corridor Committee that works with local businesses and real estate developers on the revival and economic redevelopment of the neighborhood. Cascade Village, a $50 million development, has replaced the infamous Elizabeth Park public housing project east of Howard Street with townhouses and single-family homes. Farther north, a Hickory Street housing development with access to the towpath trail is being built. And in 2007, across Howard Street from the urban park in a new arts and entertainment district, the Northside Lofts, encompassing sixty-three multistory condominiums and twenty-eight town houses, were completed. Since 2003, an annual Hot Jazz on Howard Street fundraiser is held at the former Ritz Theater with live bands, including well-known musicians who played on the street in the 1940s and 1950s. The street that Eliakim Crosby named after his son-in-law almost two centuries ago has come back to life.

The covered bridge over the canal on the Canalway Towpath Trail at Lock 11. (Bridget Garvin)

The Cascade Locks Park was a catalyst for the establishment of the Ohio & Erie National Heritage Corridor (now the Ohio & Erie National Heritage Canalway)—which extended the 21 miles of towpath trail in the Cuyahoga Valley National Park south as far as Lock 15 by the time the restoration of Mustill Store was completed. And on June 28, 2006, a new section of the towpath trail opened from Lock 15 south through the Cascade Locks Park as far as Lock 10—tripling the number of visitors to the Mustill Store.

After crossing North Street, hikers and bikers traveling south on the trail now go over a steel bridge at Lock 14, under both railroad trestles, and then over the canal on a covered bridge at Lock 11 (where the towpath crossed during the canal era)—past the sites of the mills, iron furnaces, factories, and warehouses that populated this valley during the nineteenth century. They leave the park at Beech Street, but construction of the Canalway is continuing south through downtown Akron, past Lock 1, running another 60 miles south along the route of the Ohio & Erie Canal to southern Locks 12 and 13 in Dover and New Philadelphia.

Today, Akron's Cascade Locks are on the National Register of Historic Places. They mark the site of an industrial valley that reflects the city's unique location and pay tribute to the vision of its early entrepreneurs.

POSTSCRIPT:
EXPLORING THE EXIT

Before the brick and cut stone tunnel at the north end of the Cascade Race was sealed for safety reasons, it was explored by a small group of us who realized that it probably dated from 1832 or before. We were surprised first by the quality of the workmanship. The arched entrance is comprised of alternating square stones and keystones. Some of these appear to have signature markings of the masons who built the structure. Initially, the arched stone ceiling was more than 7 feet high. But by the time the tunnel reaches its far end, 558 feet downstream, it is less than 5 feet high, suggesting that it may have been extended at a later date. The tunnel runs under North Street and under the ABTEC building before pouring its contents (which are barely a trickle today) into the Little Cuyahoga River.

The most exciting discovery made by our exploratory group was an opening about 2 feet square approximately 80 feet into the tunnel at the floor level on the west side—a square hole clogged with debris. Checking vintage maps of the Cascade Mill's hydraulics, it is apparent that the opening is opposite the bottom of the north end of the Old Mill Pit where Schumacher's 35-foot iron wheel turned and from which the effluent water from the tailrace flowed north into the Little Cuyahoga River in its own tunnel.

This opening in the side of Cascade Race tunnel suggests a possible afterthought when, perhaps, Schumacher's giant waterwheel was not

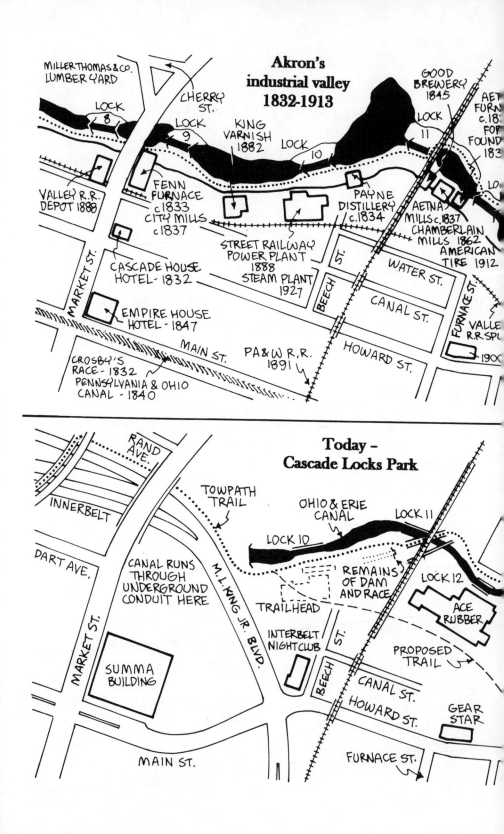

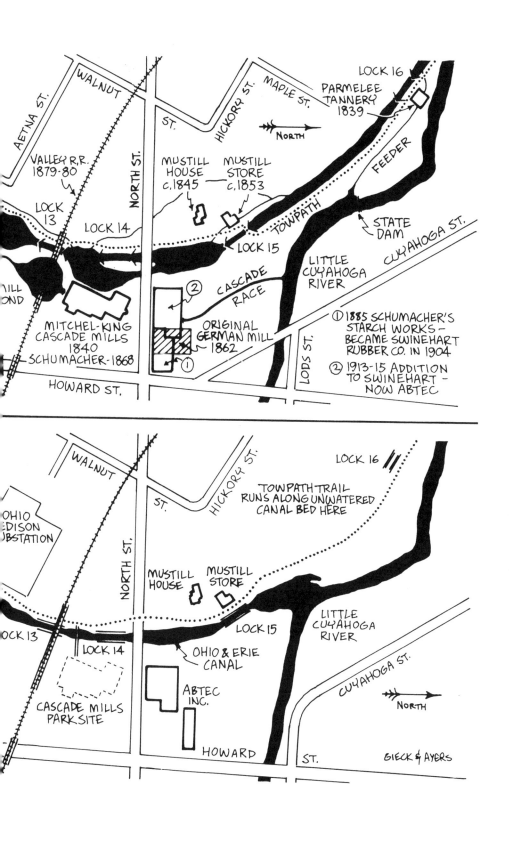

Interior of the 558-foot brick and cut stone tunnel under North Street, which carried the water from the Cascade Race to the Little Cuyahoga River. (Walter Sheppe)

generating as much power as he expected. Because the power of a waterwheel is dependent on the total fall of the water from the elevation where water enters the cups on the wheel to the depth of the tailrace into which the cups dump (which is listed on an 1880 document as 37 feet), it may have turned out that the wheel's custom tunnel didn't discharge water fast enough, so the side outlet into the Cascade Race tunnel may have been added as a solution.

The tunnel exits on the north side of ABTEC in a ditch that still flows into the Little Cuyahoga River—back into the Little Cuyahoga, after a journey of almost 3 miles from Eliakim Crosby's dam in Middlebury, down his 2-mile millrace to the edge of the Ohio & Erie Canal to turn his Old Stone Mill, then becoming the Cascade Race to power at least a dozen additional mills, factories, and furnaces, giving rise to early Akron's industrial valley and bringing the Industrial Revolution to the American Midwest.

Appendix:
Exploring the Valley

The remains of Akron's industrial valley are preserved today in Akron's Cascade Locks Park, the southern section of Cascade Valley Metro Park (one of Metro Parks, Serving Summit County). Following is a guide for visitors interested in locating the sites of some of the industries described in the preceding pages, as well as some details on each staircase of Locks 10 through 16 as they appear today. The map by Chuck Ayers will help identify these sites, as well as the many industries that operated in this part of Akron's industrial valley.

The best place to start exploring Akron's Cascade Locks Park is the **Mustill Store and Museum** at Lock 15. If you are walking the Ohio & Erie National Canalway Towpath, you can't miss its handsomely restored Greek Revival columned porch on the west side of the trail. The store is open on weekends from April through October and is free to the public. It has vintage artifacts, pictures, and models, and there are docents to show you around. For those driving to the park, the entrance to the parking lot for the Mustill Store Trailhead is on North Street. It is the third driveway to the west (right turn) from the intersection of North and Howard Streets.

The building on the northwest corner of that intersection is **ABTEC, Inc.,** which deals in recycled industrial equipment. It is on the site of Schumacher's first **German Mill,** built by Ferdinand Schumacher in the 1862 to supply oatmeal for the Union army. The mill burned in 1872 and was replaced by **Schumacher's Starch Works** in 1885. The Schumacher structure was occupied by the **Swinehart Clincher Tire & Rubber Company** in 1904. The brown brick wall facing North Street today is the south wall of the Swinehart factory built in 1913. Like many other companies in Akron, the Swinehart firm closed during the Great Depression. On the map by Chuck Ayers, the outlines of the original foundations of the three structures overlap.

(If the gate is open onto the second driveway off North Street into ABTEC's backyard, it means that local artist P. R. Miller is in residence at his outdoor gallery of avant garde metal sculptures. You will be treated to a delightful side trip if you leave your car in the Mustill Store parking lot and walk next door to see them. The free-spirited artist has created a wild and interesting assortment of colorful eccentric shapes that he fabricates from components of industrial hardware. If the gate is closed, you can still gain access [during the week] if you go to the ABTEC office inside the building.)

Across the towpath from the Mustill Store is **Lock 15**. Like all the locks in the park, it is in poor condition today. Its gates were washed out by the notorious 1913 flood.

Built during 1826 and 1827, the Cascade Locks were constructed of huge blocks of sandstone sawed and chiseled to shape. The locks all had a width of 15 feet (to permit the passage of 14-foot-wide canal boats), and they were 90 feet long. Their depth depended on the lift of the lock (from the water level above the lock to the downstream level) plus a minimum of 4 feet of water at the bottom. The lift of Lock 15 was 10 feet.

Locks were closed at both ends by heavy wooden whaler gates that closed in a V, pointing upstream so that water pressure kept them closed. Although the gates were washed away by the 1913 flood, the rectangular recesses in the lock walls into which the gates fit while open can be seen at each end.

It is apparent that the lock stones in the walls have been covered with cement. Most locks leaked from the beginning, and the leakage got worse with time as the original mortar between the lock stones disintegrated. By the end of the nineteenth century, although the only freight traffic on the Ohio & Erie was coal for the boilers of Lake Erie steamboats, there nevertheless arose a move to restore the canal to encourage an excursion trade. So, in 1906 a company called Daley Brothers was contracted to refurbish nearly all the locks between Akron and Cleveland, as well as some south of Akron. To preserve the 15-foot width of the channel, Daley workers chipped back all the sandstone blocks nearly a foot and then cast a heavy waterproofing barrier of concrete into the resulting wall cavity. They finished their project in 1907—a date the brothers left as a memento cast in cement at the south end of the lock wall. They also built many new gates, only to have their work destroyed a half-dozen years later by the 1913 flood.

Before heading south over the new towpath, it is well worth walking north about 1,000 feet down the towpath to **Lock 16.** On the way down, you will get a good look at the massive erosion created by the 1913 flood that caused the canal to pour into the Little Cuyahoga River—which is why, when you see the remains of Lock 16, you will find it is on dry land, like nearly all of the locks north of this point on the canal. Across the water you can see the Little Cuyahoga River coming in from the east and turning right at this point.

Lock 16 was deeper than Lock 15, having a lift of 11 feet—a full foot deeper than most of the Cascade Locks (see table on p. 10). You can leave the towpath and explore the lock close up here. At the north end, there is a historical marker that indicates the spot where, in 1839, Frank D. Parmelee opened a large tannery on the east side of the canal.

About halfway between Locks 15 and 16, on the east side of the towpath, are the ruins of a weir, the head of a feeder channel that added water to the canal from a dam that had been erected at this point in the Little Cuyahoga River. Its purpose was to replace canal water that had been lost upstream due to leakage and evaporation while descending through the sixteen locks below the Lock 1 summit. The channel from the river flowed into the canal below Lock 16. It was one of several such feeders from an adjacent river between Akron and Cleveland. All of the others to the north were on the Cuyahoga River, into which the Little Cuyahoga River still flows at their confluence between today's Valley View Golf Course and the Cascade Valley Park at the edge of Cuyahoga Falls.

Turning back south on the towpath, after passing the Mustill Store and Lock 15, you will see a white residence on the right side of the towpath between the store and the parking lot. This is the **Mustill House** where Fred and Emma Mustill lived from 1853 until 1888 while managing the store. The home was rehabilitated and the kitchen modernized when the store was refurbished in 2000. Occupied by a couple who maintains the historic structure, it is not open to the public.

Looking into the canal bed across from the house on the other side of the towpath, you will see tons of broken concrete and other debris that has washed down the canal waterway over the years, often in periods of high water. Some of these chunks of concrete came all the way from downtown Akron.

After crossing North Street, you will enter the recently rebuilt section of the canal towpath, which was opened in 2006 through the Cascade Locks Park from **Lock 14** through **Lock 10.** But before continuing on the towpath you will find it rewarding to turn left (east) down the sidewalk, crossing over the canal on the bridge. If you stop near the far side of the bridge and look south (upstream), you can see why these are called the Cascade Locks. And a few feet farther east, the bridge crosses the overgrown ruins of Lock 14's wasteway, or bypass channel. Every lock had one of these ditches that detoured excess water around the lock during times of less than peak traffic so that the water level wouldn't get so high that it flowed over the gates—or, worse, wash them out during a storm. Some downstream pioneer millers built lock mills that used wasteway water to power small waterwheels.

Beyond the bridge is a grassy plane to your right with a high-voltage electric tower in the background. This was the site of the Lock 14 basin, a sort of "parking lot" for canal boats waiting their turn to be loaded with barrels of flour from Cascade Mill's barrel house (or for their turn to unload coal for the adjacent powerhouse after the steam age began late in the century). In 2004–5 the foundations of both buildings were uncovered during an archaeological dig that was conducted by the University of Akron with funds raised by the Cascade Locks Park Association. (A video documentary produced during the dig is available at the Mustill Store.)

The mill buildings were in the grove of trees to the east of the basin. Farmers brought their wheat to the opposite side of the **Cascade Mill,** turning their horse-drawn wagons off Howard Street down a well-worn

The Cascade Locks looking south from North Street, with Lock 14 in the foreground. (Photo by the author)

trail about 200 feet south of North Street (near today's railroad trestle
crossing). After unloading their grist at the mill, the farmers maneu-
vered their rigs around a horseshoe turn and drove their empty wagons
back out to Howard Street.

This is where the CLPA's Planning Committee plans to build a life-sized model of Ferdinand Schumacher's huge (35-foot diameter) overshot waterwheel in its original location. (The replica, however, will be only about 18 feet high, because the lower half of the wheel was belowground.) Entrepreneur Schumacher built it this way in 1876 to maximize the fall of the water from the height from which the wheel was fed at the top to the bottom of the tailrace. The effluent stream from the tailrace ran through its own underground tunnel, which carried it under North Street and into the Little Cuyahoga River.

Going back over the bridge and heading south on the towpath, **Lock 14** will be on your left. There is a fence between the lock and the towpath. Just before the wood railing becomes a steel fence (the entrance to the footbridge), you will see an opening about 2 feet square on the opposite wall of the lock. This is the entrance to the lock's "internal sluiceway," which solved what would otherwise be a problem for boats going upstream.

Like nearly all the locks in the park, Lock 14 had a lift of 10 feet. This meant that when a boat entered through the lower gates, the butterfly valves in the upper gates were high above the boat deck; and if these were opened to fill the lock, the water gushing in from above would drench any passengers and crew who happened to be on deck below. So instead of using the butterfly valves in the upper gates to raise the boat, a wooden trapdoor over the sluiceway entrance could be slid aside and the water could go around the gate, flowing through a channel between the stones in the lock wall and coming out beside the boat below the waterline, resulting in dryer (and happier) passengers and crews. The sluiceways were needed only when a boat was going upstream. When going downstream, since the empty lock had to be filled before the boat could enter from upstream, the water levels would be equalized before the upper gates were opened. After the upper gates were closed behind the boat and the butterfly valves at the bottom of lower gates opened, the boat would ride down with the water like a hydraulic elevator as the water escaped downstream.

Crossing the canal between Lock 14 and Lock 13 is a concrete conduit encapsulating an old high-voltage electric line, one that probably dates from the 1930s. This channel points directly at an old Ohio

South end of Lock 13 (with lower railroad trestle in the background), showing the entrance to the internal sluiceway that permitted water to be bypassed
around the upper gate, coming out below the waterline of the canal boat. (Photo
by the author)

Edison manhole on the east side of the canal. It is apparent from old
maps that it also points to a corner of Schumacher's Old Mill Pit,
which housed the giant waterwheel. To the disappointment of this

writer and other researchers, however, the wheel has been long gone since the electrical lines were run. It was dismantled in 1923.

At the south end of the footbridge you will go under a steel **railroad trestle.** It is the older and lower of the two railroad bridges in the valley. This one is about 300 feet long. It spans the canal and the towpath, and is about 40 feet above the top of the lock. These dimensions make it possible to visualize the scale of Schumacher's overshot waterwheel described above: it would be just barely possible to fit that giant wheel under this trestle, not quite scraping the bottom of the bridge.

This is the second trestle built on this site. The first one was a crude-looking wooden structure seen in nineteenth-century photographs. According to Ohio railroad icon, author, and history professor Roger Grant, the wooden trestle was constructed by the Valley Line Railroad in 1879–80. This line went bankrupt in 1895 but was reorganized as the Cleveland Terminal & Valley Company the same year. The Baltimore & Ohio took control of the line in 1909. It was the B&O that built the present structure in 1931. The arched concrete piers built at that time support a steel bridge wide enough to support two tracks, but only one was laid back then, and the second pair of tracks has never been installed. It is this trestle that is crossed by today's Cuyahoga Valley Scenic Railroad, from which riders can get an aerial view of the Cascade Locks.

Coming out from under the trestle, **Lock 13** is on your left. The lock is obviously deeper than it is wide, pointing out the geometry needed to contain a minimum of 4 feet of water in the bottom plus 10 feet of lift. Embedded in concrete at the edge of this lock on the east side are the cutoff remains of power poles that were erected in the 1880s to carry electricity for one of the city's electric streetcar lines.

The concrete wall between Locks 12 and 13 was constructed by the Ohio Department of Public Works in the 1930s to contain the erosion that was developing because of the unchecked flow of water down the staircase of locks, widening the former basins and threatening to wash out lock walls. **Lock 12** is another one where the Daley Brothers left a memento of their work, with "1907" cast in concrete at the south end.

The building behind the lock is the **Ace Rubber Company,** founded by Floyd Snyder in 1935. The company is on a historic site. There were several early industries here. The first one, built more than a century earlier, was the **Aetna Furnace,** from which Furnace Street took its name. One of five cupola furnaces built along the Cascade Race during the first decade after the canal was opened, the iron foundry burned down twice and was rebuilt the second time as a flour mill known as **Aetna Mills.** In 1912, the **American Tire Company** was built on the site, joining Goodrich, Goodyear, and Firestone in serving the rapidly growing automotive industry. By 1920 the company was running on a three-shift basis, turning out 600 tires a day. But like many other Akron companies, American Tire filed for bankruptcy in 1929. The buildings remained empty until the Ace Rubber Company's founding. Snyder found that he could use American Tire's rubber-mixing equipment, which had remained in the building since American Tire's demise. At least one of the mills in the Ace mill room today bears an 1899 nameplate.

Water from the Cascade Race (still visible from the Ace property) was used by American Tire and later by Ace Rubber to cool their mills and calenders. It was used, that is, until a rail accident in downtown Akron broke open a tank car of sulfuric acid and the concentrated acid found its way into the Cascade Race, eating up Ace Rubber's pipes but, fortunately, sparing the company's mills and calenders. After that episode, owner Charles Snyder (son of the founder) not only put in new piping but revamped his plumbing so it merely recirculated water into a sump, over a spillway to cool the water, and back into the plant again. He shunted the now-questionable Cascade Race on down the hill. In continuous operation since 1935, Ace Rubber is now owned by Charles Garro, which makes decorative rubber flooring.

On the towpath you are approaching the park's still-dramatic **high trestle.** Erected in 1926 by the American Bridge Company, the lofty steel bridge over the north end of Lock 11 soars 70 feet above the lock. It is nearly 900 feet long—three times the length of the lower trestle.

Beside the towpath at Lock 12 is a historical marker displaying a picture of the predecessor of the present trestle while it was being built in 1890–91. This first trestle, an even more ethereal structure, was erected by the Pittsburgh, Akron & Western Railroad. Like the Valley Line (builder of the lower trestle at Lock 13), this railroad, too, went bankrupt in 1895.

After emerging from the south end of the covered bridge under the high trestle, you will be treated to a close-up view of the stone piers that supported the first trestle, erected here in 1890–91, standing firmly beside the path like ancient monuments. It is apparent that all the outside surfaces of the sawed sandstone blocks from which these foundation elements were built have been "brush hammered" by stonemasons to improve their professional appearance.

Looking back at the Ace Rubber complex from this vantage point, you can now see a gabled brick structure that is the oldest of the American Tire (later Ace Rubber) headquarters buildings. This is the site on which the Aetna Mill stood. Charles Snyder of Ace Rubber believed that at least some of the bricks in the back wall of this building were part of the original Aetna Mill.

It was just south of this point, between Locks 12 and 11, that twenty-seven-year-old German immigrant John T. Good opened Akron's first brewery in 1845 in partnership with fellow immigrant Michael Bittman, age sixteen.

In 1865, after taking part in the California Gold Rush, Good became Akron's first oil pioneer, opening a refinery on Furnace Street east of Lock 12. Soon tank cars of crude oil began arriving in the valley from Oil City, Pennsylvania, providing Good's distilled kerosene for Akron's oil lamps. By 1872 Good was refining 250 barrels a day, and he became one of the first exporters of lamp oil to Europe.

Having crossed the canal on the covered bridge, you return to the trail to view **Lock 11**. At its south end you can see another sluiceway entrance on the far lock wall, this one a little larger than the one at Lock 14. When the water in Lock 11 is clear, it is often possible to see the keel-protecting wooden timbers lining the bottom—surviving after nearly two centuries under water.

On your left are the **remains of a dam** preserved from the days when waterpower was the sole source of the energy that created Akron's industrial valley. Made of early concrete, dating from a time in the second half of the nineteenth century when there was only one Portland cement plant in the United States, you can see that it has two spillways, one on each side of a rectangular hydraulic box with a 48-inch opening on its north side.

Stone foundations for the 1891 steel trestle, erected by the Pittsburgh, Akron & Western Railroad, are overshadowed by the present steel structure in the background. (Photo by the author)

It was just such a dam on the Cascade Race that was the high source of the water needed to operate the overshot wheel that powered Schumacher's Cascade Mill. Attached to the north side of the 4-foot hole in the center of the dam, a ceramic pipe—a huge bell-and-spigot

Dam opposite Lock 11 (with high trestle in the background), which may have been the lofty source of water required to turn the overshot water that drove Schumacher's Cascade Mill; high trestle erected in 1926 in background. (Photo by the author)

sewer pipe—ran underground down to Schumacher's mill. Here the water rose like a siphon in a standpipe inside the mill's brick tower to feed the overshot wheel from the top. It filled the ninety-six buckets on the wheel one after the other, with the weight of the water turning the wheel three and a half times a minute (one revolution in seventeen seconds) to power all the millstones, bolting chests, sieves, and other equipment needed to grind out the product of the Cascade Mill. The Cascade Race divided into two branches upstream a few hundred yards. The other half of the stream ran parallel to the one feeding this dam to power other industries.

On the towpath, as you walk south, the trail parallels the preserved Cascade Race for a short distance before a paved path leads up the hill to the present exit at Beech Street. But it is worth walking south to the present end of the trail to see the much larger tunnel into which the canal disappears, running under the Innerbelt and staying underground through much of downtown Akron, enclosing Lock 9 through Lock 4 before reemerging at Lock 3 Plaza.

The west wall of Lock 10 has been destroyed by earlier sewer work. But on the other side of the towpath there is a historical marker between Locks 10 and 11 that invites our attention to the ruins at the top of the hill to the east:

> In 1888, the Beech Street Powerhouse was built to supply power for Akron's new electric trolleys, which replaced the city's horse-drawn street cars. Soon the plant was selling power to new businesses in downtown Akron, fueling rapid growth as the 20th century began. Ohio's infamous 1913 flood quenched the fires in the powerhouse, ending its operation. It lay dormant for 14 years until technology fueled a new use for the site—steam heat for downtown businesses.

On the marker is a large picture of the later ornate, one-story powerhouse with a single chimney, together with a color image of the multistory steam plant with its three tall smokestacks—a familiar site on Akron's northern landscape for nearly eighty years. But after standing idle for nearly half that time, the steam plant was dismantled in 2005. When a small group of us explored its interior several years ago, we learned that each of the three stacks served two steam boilers that were fed by an overhead conveyor. The conveyor was loaded with coal from a tower that housed an elevator on the south end of the building. If you exit via Beech Street, you will cross the three sets of rails for the coal cars that brought in the fuel.

Walking up the brick pavement of Beech Street toward Howard Street, you will encounter what is left of Canal Street (coming in from the left opposite the **Interbelt Nite Club**). It was at Canal and Beech Streets that David L. King built **King Varnish** in 1882, the last of the factories located in Cascade Locks Park. There were many more industries, however, along the now-buried canal remains between Lock 10 and Crosby's Mill at Lock 5.

Plans for extending the towpath are going forward. The trail will continue along the Akron Innerbelt, then bridge over it to Quaker Street (near the AT&T building). The trail section in the city's downtown is expected to be finished in the spring of 2008. It will extend along Quaker Street, turning right on Bowery and then left onto Water Street to cross State Street. Finally, it will descend into the Lock 2 area with a bridge traversing the canal to join up with the completed trail near the Canal Park baseball stadium.

The Canalway will continue past Lock 1, before running south for another 60 miles along the route of the Ohio & Erie Canal beyond Lock 1 to (south) Locks 12 and 13 in Dover and New Philadelphia. You are invited to come back and see how things are progressing.

References

Adams, John Quincy. *The Memoirs of John Quincy Adams.* 1876.

Banfield, C. W., and Kevin Beck. "The Ohio Canal, Locks 9 Through 15: A History and Study for a Proposed Archaeological Excavation." Cascade Locks Park Association, 1990.

Blower, Arthur H. *Akron at the Turn of the Century.* Akron: Summit County Historical Society, 1962.

Cascade Locks Park Association Archives.

Columbia Encyclopedia. 5th ed. New York: Columbia University Press, 1975.

Gieck, Edgar F. "Roll Call of Passenger Automobiles Produced in the United States–Canada." Unpublished manuscript, 1973. (In possession of author.)

Gieck, Jack. *Ohio's Canal Era.* Akron: Cinemark Productions DVD, 1991.

———. *A Photo Album of Ohio's Canal Era, 1825–1913.* Kent, Ohio: Kent State University Press, 1992.

———. *DIG: An Archaeological Investigation in Akron's Cascade Locks Park.* Akron Cinemark Productions DVD, 2005.

Grismer, Carl. *Akron and Summit County.* Akron: Summit County Historical Society, 1952.

Hamburg State Park. *Grist Mill Mechanics.* www.parks.org/hamburg/grist-mech.html, 2006.

Hatcher, Harlan. *The Western Reserve: The Story of New Connecticut in Ohio.* Indianapolis: Bobbs-Merrill, 1949.

Hazen, Theodore R. "The Art of Millstones and How They Work." www.angelfire.com/journal/millrestoration/millstones.html, 2006.

Hlasko, Robert A. *The Story of Ferdinand Schumacher and the Impact of the Ohio-Erie Canal on the Rise of Big Business in Akron, Ohio.* Master's thesis, University of Akron, 2003.

Howe, Henry. *Historical Collections of Ohio.* 1847.

Jackson, James S., and Margot Jackson. *The Colorful Era of the Ohio Canal.* Rev. ed. Akron: Summit County Historical Society, 1981.

Knepper, George W. *Ohio and Its People.* Kent, Ohio: Kent State University Press, 1989.

————. *Akron: City at the Summit.* 1981. Reprint. Akron: Summit County Historical Society, 1994.

Lane, Samuel A. *Fifty Years and Over of Akron and Summit County.* 1892.

Lief, Alfred. *The Firestone Story.* New York: McGraw Hill, 1951.

"Making Connections." *Cascade Chronicle* 6.3 (December 2006):1.

Maximilian, Prince of Weid's Travels in the Interior of North America, 1832–1834, ed. R. G. Thwaites. Cleveland: Arthur H. Clark Co., 1906.

Miller, Carol Poh. *Groceries, Provisions, Flour, Feed.* Akron: Cascade Locks Park Association, 1994.

Musson, Robert A. *Brewing Beer in the Buckeye State: A History of the Brewing Industry in Eastern Ohio from 1808–1904.* Medina, Ohio: Zepp Publications, 2005.

Ohio Archaeological and Historical Quarterly. 1906.

Perrin, William. *History of Summit County.* 1881.

Ravenna Western Courier and Western Public Advertiser, September 17, 1825. Archives of the Cascade Locks Park Association.

Scientific American, October, 1856.

Sears, Stephen W. *The Automobile in America.* New York: American Heritage, 1977.

Smoluk, George R. *Design News,* July 4, 1976.

Whitman, Linda G., and Anne E. Donkin. *Report[s] of the Archaeological Geophysical Survey at the Schumacher Cascade Mill Site (33Su388) in the City of Akron, Summit County, Ohio.* The University of Akron Community Archaeology Program, 2003 and 2004 [including Sanborn Insurance Company Maps, 1886, 1892, 1904].

Woods, Terry K. *The Ohio & Erie Canal: A Glossary of Terms.* Kent, Ohio: Kent State University Press, 1995.

World Book Encyclopedia. Chicago: Field Enterprises Educational Corporation, 1962.